Professional Resumes Series

RESUMES
FOR
HIGH SCHOOL
GRADUATES

The Editors of
VGM Career Horizons

VGM Career Horizons
a division of *NTC Publishing Group*
Lincolnwood, Illinois USA

Library of Congress Cataloging-in-Publication Data

Resumes for high school graduates/the editors of VGM Career
  Horizons.

    p. cm.—(VGM professional resumes series)
  ISBN 0-8442-4151-2
    1. Résumés (Employment) 2. High school graduates—Employment-
  United States. I. VGM Career Horizons (Firm) II. Series: VGM's
  professional resumes series.
  HF5383.R438 1992
  808'.06665-dc20   92-24300
                                                          CIP

Published by VGM Career Horizons, a division of NTC Publishing Group.
© 1993 by NTC Publishing Group, 4255 West Touhy Avenue,
Lincolnwood (Chicago), Illinois 60646-1975 U.S.A.

2 3 4 5 6 7 8 9 VP 9 8 7 6 5 4 3 2 1

ACKNOWLEDGMENT

The editors gratefully acknowledge Jeffrey S. Johnson and Cheryl McLean for their help in writing and production of this book.

CONTENTS

INTRODUCTION

Your resume is your first impression on a prospective employer. Though you may be articulate, intelligent, and charming in person, a poor resume may prevent you from ever having the opportunity to demonstrate your interpersonal skills, because a poor resume may prevent you from ever being called for an interview. While few people have ever been hired solely on the basis of their resume, a well-written, well-organized resume can go a long way toward helping you land an interview. Your resume's main purpose is to get you that interview. The rest is up to you and the employer. If you both feel that you are right for the job and the job is right for you, chances are you will be hired.

A resume must catch the reader's attention yet still be easy to read and to the point. Resume styles have changed over the years. Today, brief and focused resumes are preferred. No longer do employers have the patience, or the time, to review two or three pages of solid type. A resume should be only one page long, if possible, and never more than two pages. Time is a precious commodity in today's business world and the resume that is concise and straightforward will usually be the one that gets noticed.

Let's not make the mistake, though, of assuming that writing a brief resume means that you can take less care in preparing it. A successful resume takes time and thought, and if you are willing to make the effort, the rewards are well worth it. Think of your resume as a sales tool with the product being you. You want to sell yourself to a prospective employer. This book is designed to help you prepare a resume that will help you further your career—to land that next job, or first job, or to return to the work force after years of absence. So, read on. Make the effort and reap the rewards that a strong resume can bring to your career. Let's get to it!

Chapter One

THE ELEMENTS OF A GOOD RESUME

A winning resume is made of the elements that employers are most interested in seeing when reviewing a job applicant. These basic elements are the ingredients of a successful resume and are essential to any resume. These elements become the actual sections of your resume. The following is a list of elements that may be used in a resume. Some are essential; some are optional. We will be discussing these in this chapter in order to give you a better understanding of each element's role in the makeup of your resume:

1. Heading
2. Objective
3. Work Experience
4. Education
5. Licenses and Certificates
6. Professional Memberships
7. Honors
8. Activities
9. Special Skills
10. References

The first step in preparing your resume is to gather together all the information about yourself and your past accomplishments.

Later you will refine this information, rewrite it in the most effective language, and organize it into the most attractive layout. First, let's take a look at each of these important elements individually.

Heading

The heading may seem to be a simple enough element in your resume, but be careful not to take it lightly. The heading should be placed at the top of your resume and should include your name, home address, and telephone numbers. If you can take calls at your current place of business, include your business number, since most employers will attempt to contact you during the business day. If this is not possible, or if you can afford it, purchase an answering machine that allows you to retrieve your messages while you are away from home. This way you can make sure you don't miss important phone calls. *Always* include your phone number on your resume. It is crucial that when prospective employers need to have immediate contact with you, they can.

Objective

When seeking a particular career path, it is important to list a job objective on your resume. This statement helps employers know the direction that you see yourself heading, so that they can determine whether your goals are in line with the position available. The objective is normally one sentence long and describes your employment goals clearly and concisely.

Below are a few examples of job objectives as they might appear on a resume:

Example #1

OBJECTIVE: To join a small- to medium-sized public accounting firm with a near-term goal of partnership admission.

Example #2

OBJECTIVE: To secure a position as a paralegal where I can utilize my education, my writing, and my interpersonal skills.

Example #3

OBJECTIVE: A professional sales position, leading to management in the food industry, where my administrative experience, communications skills, and initiative can be utilized to increase sales and improve customer relations.

As you can see, the job objective will vary depending on the type of person you are and the type of goals you have. It can be either specific or general, but it should always be to the point.

This element in some cases is not necessary, but usually it is a good idea to include your objective. It gives your possible future employer an idea of where you are coming from and where you want to go.

Work Experience

This element is arguably the most important of them all. It will provide the central focus of your resume, so it is necessary that this section be as complete as possible. Only by examining your work experience in depth can you get to the heart of your accomplishments and present them in a way that demonstrates the strength of your qualifications. Of course, someone just out of school will have less work experience than someone who has been working for a number of years, but the amount of information isn't the most important thing—rather, how it is presented and how it highlights you as a person and as a worker will be what counts.

As you work on this section of your resume, be aware of the need for accuracy. You'll want to include all necessary information about each of your jobs, including job title, dates, employer, city, state, responsibilities, special projects, and accomplishments. Be sure to only list company accomplishments for which you were directly responsible. If you haven't participated in any special projects, that's all right—this area may not be relevant to certain jobs.

A basic rule of resume writing, and an extremely important one is: *List all work experience in reverse chronological order.* In other words, always start with your most recent job and work your way backwards. This way your prospective employer sees your current (and usually most important) job before seeing your less important past jobs. Your most recent position should also be the one that includes the most information, as compared to your previous positions. If you are just out of school, show your summer employment and part-time work, though your education will most likely be more important than your work experience in this case.

The following worksheets will help you gather information about your past jobs. Begin with your most recent job and work backwards.

WORK EXPERIENCE
Job One:

Job Title _____

Dates _____

Employer _____

City, State _____

Major Duties _____

_____

_____

_____

_____

_____

_____

Special Projects _____

_____

_____

_____

Accomplishments _____

_____

_____

_____

_____

_____

_____

_____

Job Two:

Job Title _____

Dates _____

Employer _____

City, State _____

Major Duties _____

_____

_____

_____

_____

_____

_____

_____

Special Projects _____

_____

_____

_____

Accomplishments _____

_____

_____

_____

_____

_____

_____

_____

_____

_____

Job Three:

Job Title _____

Dates _____

Employer _____

City, State _____

Major Duties _____

_____

_____

_____

_____

_____

_____

Special Projects _____

_____

_____

Accomplishments _____

_____

_____

_____

_____

_____

_____

_____

Job Four:

Job Title _____

Dates _____

Employer _____

City, State _____

Major Duties _____

_____

_____

_____

_____

_____

_____

Special Projects _____

_____

_____

_____

Accomplishments _____

_____

_____

_____

_____

_____

_____

_____

_____

Education

Education is the second most important element of a resume. Your educational background is often a deciding factor in an employer's decision to hire you. Be sure to stress your accomplishments in school with the same finesse that you stressed your accomplishments at work. If you are looking for your first job, your education will be your greatest asset, since your work experience will most likely be minimal. In this case, the education section becomes the most important. You will want to be sure to include any degrees or certificates you received, your major area of concentration, any honors, and any relevant activities. Again, be sure to list your most recent schooling first.

The following worksheets will help you gather information for this section of your resume. Also included are supplemental worksheets for honors and for activities. Sometimes honors and activities are listed in a section separate from education, most often near the end of the resume.

EDUCATION

School _____

Major or Area of Concentration _____

Degree _____

Date _____

School _____

Major or Area of Concentration _____

Degree _____

Date _____

School _____

Major or Area of Concentration _____

Degree _____

Date _____

Honors

Here, you should list any awards, honors, or memberships in honorary societies that you have received. Usually these are of an academic nature, but they can also be for special achievement in sports, clubs, or other school activities. Always be sure to include the name of the organization honoring you and the date(s) received, e.g., Dean's List, 1989, 1990. Use the worksheet below to help gather your honors information.

HONORS

Honor: _____

Awarding Organization: _____

Date(s): _____

Honor: _____

Awarding Organization: _____

Date(s): _____

Honor: _____

Awarding Organization: _____

Date(s): _____

Honor: _____

Awarding Organization: _____

Date(s): _____

Activities

You may have been active in different organizations or clubs during your years at school; often an employer will look at such involvement as evidence of initiative and dedication. Your ability to take an active role, and even a leadership role, in a group should be included on your resume. Use the worksheet provided to list your activities and accomplishments in this area.

ACTIVITIES

Organization/Activity: _____

Accomplishments: _____

_____

_____

Organization/Activity: _____

Accomplishments: _____

_____

_____

Organization/Activity: _____

Accomplishments: _____

_____

_____

Organization/Activity: _____

Accomplishments: _____

_____

_____

As your work experience increases through the years, your school activities and honors will play less of a role in your resume, and eventually you will most likely only list your degree and any major honors you received. This is due to the fact that, as time goes by, your job performance becomes the most important element in your resume. So, through time your resume should change to reflect this.

Certificates and Licenses

The next potential element of your resume is certificates and licenses. You should list these if the job you are seeking requires them and you, of course, have acquired them. If you have applied for a license, but have not yet received it, use the phrase "application pending."

License requirements vary by state. If you have moved or you are planning to move to another state, be sure to check with the appropriate board or licensing agency in the state in which you are applying for work to be sure that you are aware of all the necessary requirements.

Always be sure that all of the information you list is completely accurate. Locate copies of your licenses and certificates and check the exact date and name of the accrediting agency, e.g., Teaching Certificate, State of Illinois Board of Education, 1988. Use the following worksheet to list your licenses and certificates.

CERTIFICATES AND LICENSES

Name of License: _____

Licensing Agency: _____

Date Issued: _____

Name of License: _____

Licensing Agency: _____

Date Issued: _____

Name of License: _____

Licensing Agency: _____

Date Issued: _____

Professional Memberships

Another potential element in your resume is a section that lists professional memberships. Use this section to list any involvement in professional associations, unions, and similar organizations. It is to your advantage to list any professional memberships that pertain to the job you are seeking. Be sure to include the dates of your involvement and whether you took part in any special activities or held any offices within the organization, e.g., Society of Civil Engineers, 1986–present. Use the following worksheet to gather your information.

PROFESSIONAL MEMBERSHIPS

Name of Organization: _____

Offices Held: _____

Activities: _____

Date(s): _____

Name of Organization: _____

Offices Held: _____

Activities: _____

Date(s): _____

Name of Organization: _____

Offices Held: _____

Activities: _____

Date(s): _____

Name of Organization: _____

Offices Held: _____

Activities: _____

Date(s): _____

Special Skills

This section of your resume is set aside for mentioning any special abilities you have that could relate to the job you are seeking. Today, many employers seek applicants who have experience with computers. Be sure to list all types of computer hardware and software with which you have familiarity. Often, knowledge of a particular type of software is essential if the company you are interviewing with uses it exclusively. This is the part of your resume where you have the opportunity to demonstrate certain talents and experiences that are not necessarily a part of your educational or work experience.

Another beneficial special skill is knowledge of a foreign language. Just open a newspaper to the classified section, and you will notice the numerous job openings for those with bilingual skills. Be sure to mention if you are fluent or simply have a working knowledge of a foreign language. This will make a difference to your employer.

Special skills can encompass a wide range of your talents—from being a freelance editor to being an expert pilot. Remember to be sure that whatever skills you list relate directly or indirectly to the type of work you are looking for.

References

References are not usually listed on the resume, but a prospective employer needs to know that you have references who may be contacted if necessary. All that is necessary to include in your resume regarding references is a sentence at the bottom stating, "References are available upon request." This will suffice. A prospective employer may indeed wish to have a list of references, so be sure to have your list ready before you send out your resume. Also, check with whomever you list to see if it is all right for you to use them as a reference. Forewarn them that they may receive a call regarding a reference for you. This way they can be prepared to give you the best reference possible.

Chapter Two

WRITING YOUR RESUME

*N*ow that you have gathered together all of the information for each of the sections of your resume, it's time to write out each section in a way that will get the attention of whoever is reviewing it. The type of language you use in your resume has a profound effect on its success. You want to take the information you have gathered and translate it into a language that will cause a potential employer to sit up and take notice.

Resume writing is not like expository writing or creative writing. It embodies a functional, direct writing style and focuses on the use of action words. By using action words in your writing, you more effectively stress past accomplishments. Action words help demonstrate your initiative and highlight your talents. Always use verbs that show strength and reflect the qualities of a "doer." For example, instead of "Put together a sales plan for the Midwest," use "Orchestrated a regional sales plan that increased sales in several midwestern states." Instead of "The newspaper was redesigned while I was managing editor," say "Served as managing editor. Redesigned newspaper's layout." By using action words, you characterize yourself as a person who takes action, and this will impress potential employers.

The following is a list of verbs commonly used in resume writing. Note that it is resume style to use the past tense (*-ed*) rather that the present. Use this list to choose the action words that can help your resume become a strong one:

administered	introduced
advised	invented
analyzed	maintained
arranged	managed
assembled	met with
assumed responsibility	motivated
billed	negotiated
built	operated
carried out	orchestrated
channeled	ordered
collected	organized
communicated	oversaw
compiled	performed
completed	planned
conducted	prepared
contacted	presented
contracted	produced
coordinated	programmed
counseled	published
created	purchased
cut	recommended
designed	recorded
determined	reduced
developed	referred
directed	represented
dispatched	researched
distributed	reviewed
documented	saved
edited	screened
established	served as
expanded	served on
functioned as	sold
gathered	suggested
handled	supervised
hired	taught
implemented	tested
improved	trained
inspected	typed
interviewed	wrote

Now let's take a look at the information you put down on the work experience worksheets. Take that information and rewrite it in paragraph form, using verbs to highlight your actions and accomplishments. Let's look at an example:

WORK EXPERIENCE

Job Title: Regional Sales Manager

Dates: 1988–1992

Employer: Pillsbury & Co.

City, State: Levittown, PA

Major Duties: Manager of sales representatives from seven states. Responsible for twelve food chain accounts in the east. In charge of directing the sales force in planned selling toward specific goals. Supervisor and trainer of new sales representatives. Consulting for customers in the areas of inventory management and quality control.

Special Projects: Coordinator and sponsor of annual food industry sales seminar.

Accomplishments: Monthly regional volume went up 25 percent during my tenure while, at the same time, a proper sales/cost ratio was maintained. Customer/company relations improved significantly.

Below is the rewritten version of this information, using action words. Notice how much stronger it sounds.

WORK EXPERIENCE

Pillsbury & Co., Levittown, PA

Regional Sales Manager, 1988–1992

Managed sales representatives from seven states. Handled twelve food chain accounts in the eastern United States. Directed the sales force in planned selling towards specific goals. Supervised and trained new sales representatives. Consulted for customers in the areas of inventory management and quality control. Coordinated and sponsored the annual Food Industry Seminar. Increased monthly regional volume 25 percent and helped to improve customer/company relations during my tenure.

This is the kind of direct, strong language necessary for a successful resume. Another way of constructing the work experience section is by using actual job descriptions. Job descriptions are rarely written using the proper resume language, but they do include all the information necessary to create this section of your resume. Take the description of one of the jobs you are including on your resume (if you have access to it), and turn it into an action-oriented paragraph. Below is an example of a job description followed by a version of the same description written using action words.

PUBLIC ADMINISTRATOR I

Responsibilities: Coordinate and direct public services to meet the needs of the nation, state, or community. Analyze problems; work with special committees and public agencies; recommend solutions to governing bodies.

Aptitudes and Skills: Ability to relate to and communicate with people; solve complex problems through analysis; plan, organize, and implement policies and programs. Knowledge of political systems; financial management; personnel administration; program evaluation; organizational theory.

WORK EXPERIENCE
State of California, Los Angeles, California

Public Administrator I, 1985–1990

Wrote pamphlets and conducted discussion groups to inform citizens of legislative processes and consumer issues. Organized and supervised crew of interviewers. Trained interviewers in effective communication skills.

Now that you have learned how to word your resume, you are ready for the next step in your quest for a winning resume: assembly and layout.

Chapter Three

ASSEMBLY AND LAYOUT

*A*t this point, you've gathered all the necessary information for your resume, and you've rewritten it using the language necessary to impress potential employers. Your next step is to assemble these elements in a logical order and then to lay them out on the page neatly and attractively in order to achieve the desired effect: getting that interview.

Assembly

The order of the elements in a resume makes a difference in its overall effect. Obviously, you would not want to put your name and address in the middle of the resume or your special skills section at the top. You want to put the elements in an order that stresses your most important achievements, not the less pertinent information. For example, if you recently graduated from school and have no full-time work experience, you will want to list your education before you list any part-time jobs you may have held during school. On the other hand, if you have been gainfully employed for several years and currently hold an important position in your company, you will want to list your work experience ahead of your education, which has become less pertinent with time.

There are some elements that are always included in your resume and some that are optional. On page 20 is a list of essential and optional elements:

Essential	*Optional*
Name	Job Objective
Address	Honors
Phone Number	Special Skills
Work Experience	Professional Memberships
Education	Activities
References Phrase	Certificates and Licenses

Your choice of optional sections depends on your own background and employment needs. Always use information that will put you and your abilities in a favorable light. If your honors are impressive, then be sure to include them in your resume. If your activities in school demonstrate particular talents necessary for the job you are seeking, then allow space for a section on activities. Each resume is unique, just as each person is unique.

Types of Resumes

So far, our discussion about resumes has involved the most common type—the *chronological resume*. In a chronological resume, all work experience is listed in reverse chronological order, with your most recent job first and so on. This is the type of resume usually preferred by human resources directors, and it is the one most frequently used. However, in some cases this style of presentation is not the most effective way to highlight your skills and accomplishments.

For someone reentering the work force after many years or someone looking to change career fields, the *functional resume* may work best. This type of resume focuses more on achievement and less on the sequence of your work history. In the functional resume, your experience is presented by what you have accomplished and the skills you have developed in your past work.

A functional resume can be assembled from the same information you collected for your chronological resume. The main difference lies in the use you make of this information. Essentially, the work experience section becomes two sections, with your job duties and accomplishments comprising one section and your employer's name, city, state, your position, and the dates employed making up another section. The first section is placed near the top of the resume, just below the job objective section, and can be called *Accomplishments* or *Achievements*. The second section, containing the bare essentials of your employment history, should come after the accomplishments section and can be titled *Work Experience* or *Employment History*. The other sections of your resume remain the same. The work experience section is the only one affected in the functional resume. By placing the section that focuses on your achievements first, you thereby draw attention to these achievements. This puts less emphasis on who you worked for and more emphasis on what you did and what you are capable of doing.

For someone changing careers, emphasis on skills and achievements is essential. The identities of previous employers, which may be unrelated to one's new job field, need to be downplayed. The functional resume accomplishes this task. For someone reentering the work force after many years, a functional resume is the obvious choice. If you lack full-time work experience, you will need to draw attention away from this fact and instead focus on your skills and abilities gained possibly through volunteer activities or part-time work. Education may also play a more important role in this resume.

Which type of resume is right for you will depend on your own personal circumstances. It may be helpful to create a chronological *and* a functional resume and then compare the two to find out which is more suitable. The sample resumes found in this book include both chronological and functional resumes. Use these resumes as guides to help you decide on the content and appearance of your own resume. One example each of chronological and functional resumes follows on the next two pages.

Layout

Once you have decided which elements to include in your resume and you have arranged them in an order that makes sense and emphasizes your achievements and abilities, then it is time to work on the physical layout of your resume.

There is no single appropriate layout that applies to every resume, but there are a few basic rules to follow in putting your resume on paper:

1. Leave a comfortable margin on the sides, top, and bottom of the page (usually 1 to 1½ inches).

2. Use appropriate spacing between the sections (usually 2 to 3 line spaces are adequate).

3. Be consistent in the *type* of headings you use for the different sections of your resume. For example, if you capitalize the heading EMPLOYMENT HISTORY, don't use initial capitals and underlining for a heading of equal importance, such as Education.

4. Always try to fit your resume onto one page. If you are having trouble fitting all your information onto one page, perhaps you are trying to say too much. Try to edit out any repetitive or unnecessary information or possibly shorten descriptions of earlier jobs. Maybe

CHRONOLOGICAL RESUME

DAVID P. JENKINS
3663 N. Coldwater Canyon
North Hollywood, CA 90390
818/555-3472
818/555-3678

JOB OBJECTIVE: A position as a sales/marketing manager where I can ultilize
my knowledge and experience by combining high volume selling
of major accounts with an administrative ability that increases
sales through encouragement of sales team.

EMPLOYMENT
HISTORY:

Tribor Industries, Los Angeles, CA
Regional Sales Manager, 1985 - present
Managed sales of all product lines in western markets for a
leading maker of linens. Represented five corporate divisions
of the company with sales in excess of $3,000,000 annually.
Directed and motivated a sales force of 12 sales representatives
in planned selling to achieve company goals.

Tribor Industries, Los Angeles, CA
District Manager, 1980 - 1985
Acted as sales representive for the Los Angeles metropolitan
area. Built both wholesale and dealer distribution substantially
during my tenure. Promoted to Regional Sales Manager after five
years service.

American Office Supply, Chicago, IL
Assisant to Sales Manager, 1976 - 1980
Handled both internal and external areas of sales and marketing,
including samples, advertising and pricing. Served as company
sales representative and sold a variety of office supplies to
retail stores.

EDUCATION: **University of Michigan**, Ann Arbor, MI
B.A. Business Administration, 1975
Major Field: Management

SEMINARS: National Management Association Seminar, 1984
Purdue University Seminars, 1987, 1988

PROFESSIONAL
MEMBERSHIPS: Sales and Marketing Association of Los Angeles
National Association of Market Developers

REFERENCES: Available upon request

FUNCTIONAL RESUME

SARA WOODS
4400 Sunset Blvd.
Los Angeles, CA 90028
213/555-8989
213/555-6666

OBJECTIVE: A position in sales management.

ACHIEVEMENTS: * Planned successful strategies to identify and develop new accounts.
                * Increased sales by at least 20% each year as District Sales
                  Manager.
                * Researched and analyzed market conditions in order to seek out
                  new customers.
                * Developed weekly and monthly sales strategies.
                * Supervised seven sales representatives.
                * Conducted field visits to solve customer complaints.
                * Maintained daily customer contact to insure good customer/
                  company relations.
                * Wrote product information fliers and distributed them through
                  a direct mail program.

WORK
EXPERIENCE: Southern California Fruit Co., Los Angeles, CA
                District Sales Manager, 1986 - present

                L.A. Freight Co., Los Angeles, CA
                Account Executive, 1984 - 1986

                Handlemen & Associates, Santa Rita, CA
                Sales Representative, 1983 - 1984

EDUCATION: University of Colorado, Boulder, CO
                B.A., 1983
                Major: Management
                Minor: Political Science
                G.P.A. 3.3/4.0

PROFESSIONAL
MEMBERSHIPS: Southern California Sales Association, Treasurer, 1988 - 1990
                Los Angeles Chamber of Commerce, 1986 - present

SPECIAL
SKILLS: DOS experience. LOTUS/DBASE/WORD PERFECT experience.

REFERENCES: Provided on request

you've included too many optional sections. Don't let the idea of having to tell every detail about your life get in the way of producing a resume that is simple and straightforward. The more compact your resume, the easier it will be to read and the better impression it will make for you.

Try experimenting with various layouts until you find one that looks good to you. It may be a good idea to show your final layout to people who can tell you what they think is right or wrong with it. Ask them what impresses them most about your resume. Make sure that is what you want most to emphasize. If it isn't, you may want to consider making changes in your layout until the necessary information is emphasized. Use the sample resumes in chapter 5 to get some ideas for laying out your resume.

Putting Your Resume in Print

Your resume should be typed or printed on good quality 8½" × 11" bond paper. You want to make as good an impression as possible with your resume; therefore, quality paper is a necessity. If you have access to a word processor with a good printer, make use of it. If not, a typewriter that produces good, clean copy should be just fine.

After you have produced a clean original, you will want to go ahead and make duplicate copies of it. Usually a copy shop is your best bet for producing copies without smudges or streaks. Make sure you have the copy shop use quality bond paper for all copies of your resume. Ask for a sample copy before they run your entire order. After copies are made, check each copy for cleanliness and clarity.

Another more costly option is to have your resume typeset and printed by a printer. This will provide the most attractive resume, but most likely the neat, clean, hand-typed resume will have the same effect as the typeset resume at far less expense.

Proofreading

After you have finished typing the master copy of your resume and before you go to have it copied or printed, you must thoroughly check it for typing and spelling errors. Have several people read it over just in case you may have missed an error. Misspelled words and typing mistakes will not make a good impression on a prospective employer. They are a bad reflection on your writing ability and your attention to detail. With thorough and conscientious proofreading, these mistakes can be avoided. The following are some rules of capitalization and punctuation that may come in handy when proofreading your resume:

Rules of Capitalization

- Capitalize proper nouns, such as names of schools, colleges and universities, names of companies, and brand names of products.
- Capitalize major words in the names and titles of books, tests, and articles that appear in the body of your resume.
- Capitalize words in major section headings of your resume.
- Do not capitalize words just because they seem important.
- When in doubt, consult a manual of style such as *Words Into Type* (Prentice-Hall); or *The Chicago Manual of Style*, (The University of Chicago Press). Your local library can help you locate these and others.

Rules of Punctuation

- Use a comma to separate words in a series.
- Use a semicolon to separate series of words that already include commas within the series.
- Use a semicolon to separate independent clauses that are not joined by a conjunction.
- Use a period to end a sentence.
- Use a colon to show that the examples or details that follow expand or amplify the preceding phrase.
- Avoid the use of dashes.
- Avoid the use of brackets.
- If you use any punctuation in an unusual way in your resume, be consistent in its use.
- Whenever you are uncertain, consult a style manual.

Chapter Four

THE COVER LETTER

*O*nce your resume has been assembled, laid out, and printed to your satisfaction, the next and final step before distribution is to write your cover letter. Though there may be instances where you deliver your resume in person, most often you will be sending it through the mail. Resumes sent through the mail always need an accompanying letter that briefly introduces you and your resume. The purpose of the cover letter is to get a potential employer to read your resume, just as the purpose of your resume is to get that same potential employer to call you for an interview.

Like your resume, your cover letter should be clean, neat, and direct. A cover letter usually includes the following information:

1. Your name and address (unless it already appears on your personal letterhead).

2. The date.

3. The name and address of the person and company to whom you are sending your resume.

4. The salutation ("Dear Mr." or "Dear Ms." followed by the person's last name, or "To Whom It May Concern" if you are answering a blind ad).

5. An opening paragraph explaining why you are writing (in response to an ad, the result of a previous meeting, at the suggestion of someone you both know) and indicating that you are interested in whatever job is being offered.

6. One or two more paragraphs that tell why you want to work for the company and what qualifications and experience you can bring to that company.

7. A final paragraph that closes the letter and requests that you be contacted for an interview.

8. The closing ("Sincerely," or "Yours Truly," followed by your signature with your name typed under it).

Your cover letter, including all of the information above, should be no more than one page in length. The language used should be polite, businesslike, and to the point. Do not attempt to tell your life story in the cover letter. A long and cluttered letter will only serve to put off the reader. Remember, you only need to mention a few of your accomplishments and skills in the cover letter. The rest of your information is in your resume. Each and every achievement does not need to be mentioned twice. If your cover letter is a success, your resume will be read and all pertinent information reviewed by your prospective employer.

Producing The Cover Letter

Cover letters should always be typed individually, since they are always written to particular individuals and companies. Never use a form letter for your cover letter. Cover letters cannot be copied or reproduced like resumes. Each one should be as personal as possible. Of course, once you have written and rewritten your first cover letter to the point where you are satisfied with it, you certainly can use similar wording in subsequent letters.

After you have typed your cover letter on quality bond paper, be sure to proofread it as thoroughly as you did your resume. Again, spelling errors are a sure sign of carelessness, and you don't want that to be a part of your first impression on a prospective employer. Make sure to handle the letter and resume carefully to avoid any smudges, and then mail both your cover letter and resume in an appropriate sized envelope. Be sure to keep an accurate record of all the resumes you send out and the results of each mailing.

Numerous sample cover letters appear at the end of the book. Use them as models for your own cover letter or to get an idea of how cover letters are put together. Remember, every one is unique and depends on the particular circumstances of the individual writing it.

Now your job is complete. You can let your cover letter and resume do the rest and land you that interview that very well could lead to the job you are seeking.

Chapter Five

SAMPLE RESUMES

This chapter contains dozens of sample resumes for people pursuing a wide variety of jobs and careers. There are many different styles of resumes in terms of graphic layout and presentation of information. These samples also represent people with varying amounts of education and work experience. Use these samples to model your own resume after. Choose one resume, or borrow elements from several different resumes to help you construct your own.

Andrew G. Meunier
6300 Beasley Road
Jackson, Mississippi 39225
601/555-7819

Personal Objective   Job with automotive repair or body shop.

Experience   **Automotive Repair and Body Work**

- Assisted with complete exterior repair of six cars.
- Assisted in engine rebuild and repair.
- Detail painting on two vans.
- Interior work on several vans.

Home Maintenance

- Provided landscaping maintenance for apartment complex.
- Interior and exterior painting of two homes.
- Assisted with roofing of one new home and repair on another.
- Minor carpentry work for apartment complex.

Work History   Handyman   1991-present
Delta Apartments
2400 Albermarle Road
Jackson, MS 39213
Supervisor: Adrian Florio

Duties: landscape maintenance, carpentry, general repair.

Custodian   1990-1991
Alternative Junior High School
1900 N. State Street
Jackson, MS 39202
Supervisor: Johnson Ableman

Duties: sweeping, vacuuming, cleaning restrooms, basic janitorial work.

Skills & Activities   Sign language, drawing, and painting. Member of Car Rally Club of Jackson, Boy Scouts of America (Eagle Scout)

Education   Wingfield Senior High School, 1985 Scanlon Drive, Jackson, MS
Diploma received June 1992

Courses: auto mechanics I & II; wood shop I & II; Spanish II & III.

References   Available on request

LaToya Cook

512 Lynn Road, Excelsior Springs, MO 64024   816/555-3225

Personal Goal

A position involving writing and editing.

Experience

Editor, *The Easterly Breeze* (student newspaper)

• Wrote series on racial integration programs in Missouri high schools that won a state Junior Journalist award in 1991 from the Missouri Association of Newspaper Journalists. One article from the series was published in the MANJ newsletter.

• Write monthly column about student life and issues at East High School.

• Interview teachers and students for personality profile articles for publication in the student newspaper.

• Edit stories written by other students for spelling, grammar, and AP news style.

Reporter, *Encounters* (student yearbook)

• Wrote articles on sports for publication in yearbook.

• Wrote captions for photographs.

• Assisted staff photographers with taking group photographs.

Education

East High School
101 Richmond Street
Excelsior Springs, MO 64024
9/89 - 6/93
Current GPA: 3.75

Pertinent Courses: Journalism, Photography, Honors English (three years), Intro to Law, American Government

References

Available on request

Shawna Udey

2354 S.E. Grand Avenue
Billings, Montana 59105
(406) 555-5835

Job Desired

Preschool or day care center teaching assistant.

Work Experience

6/91-present

Childcare, Faubian Elementary School
3039 N.E. Sierra Boulevard
Billings, MT 59102
(406) 255-5085
Supervisor: Nancy Toppila

Duties: Provide childcare during adult education parenting classes.

6/90-present

Volunteer, St. Vincent's Hospital
2915 Twelfth Avenue
Billings, MT 59101
(406) 254-2333
Supervisor: Jamilla de Corazon, R.N.

Duties: Worked as candy striper, providing reading material, reading aloud, visiting with patients, and assisting nurses.

Education

9/89 – 6/93

Skyview High School, 1775 High Sierra Boulevard, Billings

Related Coursework:
One year each: Child Development, Teacher Assistant, Home Economics and Nutrition, Health and Fitness

Related Skills

• Hold CPR and basic emergency first aid certification
• Trained in babysitting by Yellowstone County Red Cross
• Completed courses in infant care at St. Vincent's Hospital

References on request

Estrella Angelino
2240 W. Yucca Street
Santa Fe, New Mexico 87538
(505) 555-5121

Objective   Finding a challenging part-time job in sales and customer service with opportunity for future advancement.

Relevant Training

- Typing I-II
- English I-III
- Finance and accounting I-II

- Office systems & procedures
- Computer applications I-II
- Computer accounting

Education

Capital High School, Santa Fe. Diploma, June 1992.

Work Experience

Square Pan Pizza, Paseo del Sol, Santa Fe
(Hired April 1991; store closed December 1991)

My responsibilities included greeting customers, taking orders, handling cash, operating the register, answering telephones, cooking, cleaning, and assisting with closing.

The Bite of Santa Fe
(Volunteer in 1989, 1990, 1991)
I served as a volunteer for the city's annual weekend celebration of food and music in downtown Santa Fe. Duties in 1989 and 1990 included working with the public, taking orders, handling cash, and serving ice cream. In 1991 I served soda drinks and handled cash.

St. Vincent de Paul, Santa Fe
(Volunteer since 1991)
I worked as a volunteer helping serve food and distribute clothing and supplies to people in need.

References available on request

Alexander Hyde Branch III
Rural Route 01, Box 43B
Geneva, Nebraska 68361
(402) 555-2822

Job Desired	Bank teller or bank clerk with opportunities for utilizing my education in finance and accounting.

Education

9/89 – present	Geneva North High School Rural Route 01, Box 23A Geneva, Nebraska 68361 Major: Business

Experience	Completed series of accounting courses that involved recording and analyzing financial transactions, developing financial plans, and preparing financial statements.
	Learned computer-assisted accounting using two different software programs, ACCPAC Plus and Lotus 1-2-3.
	Participated in class-run simulated business as financial manager. Developed business plan and worked with marketing manager to carry out business objectives.
	Participated in career visitations to a variety of financial institutions.

Activities	Vice president, Future Business Leaders of America Member, DECA (marketing club) Reporter on student newspaper Treasurer, National Honor Society

Work History

5/91 – present	Burger King 366 N.W. Frontage Geneva, Nebraska 68361 Supervisor: Bobbie Mahew
	Duties: As a line cashier, I greet customers, take orders, prepare food, handle cash, and balance receipts against sales at the end of my shift. I have never been late to work or missed a day. Chosen as Cashier of the Month July 1991.

References	Available upon request

PATRICIA FINLEY

351 N. 22nd • Las Vegas, Nevada 89102 • (702) 555-1377

JOB GOALS

Entry-level position in bank or bookkeeping firm.

EDUCATION

Clark Senior High School, 4291 Pennwood Avenue, Las Vegas
Expected graduation date: 1993

Courses of Study:
Three years Math, Accounting II, Computer Systems; currently enrolled in Japanese I, Advanced Algebra, and serving as a Teacher Assistant.

EXPERIENCE

• Experienced with payroll reports and bookkeeping. Studied federal and state payroll tax guidelines and prepared quarterly reports. Assumed responsibility for three small-business accounts, maintaining income and expense ledgers and providing monthly statements.

• Experienced with general ledger accounting on ACCPAC software.

• For the marketing club, I served as Treasurer and was responsible for maintaining the sales and expenses records for the Student Store.

WORK HISTORY

• Finley & Associates, CPAs, Las Vegas. Summers 1990-present.

ACTIVITIES

• Portfolio Club: Earned 27 percent on investments made in mock stock market investment program for business students.

• Marketing Club Treasurer: Elected from among 82 student members; attended regional convention in Santa Fe, New Mexico, to represent our chapter's school store program innovations.

• National Honor Society / School Honor Roll

• Spanish Club. Helped plan club-sponsored field trips and a Spanish banquet to raise funds for a trip to Mexico.

REFERENCES

• Available on request

Marshall L. Floyd

2825 Evans Avenue, Suncook, New Hampshire 03275 / 555-9941

Professional Goal   Summer assistant to state legislator.

Education

1989-present	Pembroke Academy, Suncook, New Hampshire
	Expected graduation date: 1993
1987-1988	Exeter School for Boys, Exeter, New Hampshire

Relevant Courses
- American Government
- Business Law
- Western Civilization
- World History
- Sociology

Work Experience

June-August 1991   Briscoe and Havering, Attorneys at Law, Manchester, New Hampshire

Duties: Worked with attorneys and legal assistants to gather documentation needed for litigation proceedings. Assisted with research, maintained legal library records, and obtained necessary materials from central law library at the college.

Skills
- Experienced with computers (Word Perfect, dBase on IBM)
- Good research skills
- Typing, 45 w.p.m.

Activities
- Went to state competition as a member of Model United Nations (Greece)
- Member of Future Business Leaders of America
- Served as Outdoor School Junior Counselor for three sessions
- Coached Junior Soccer for the Boys & Girls Club of Merrimack County

References   Available on request.

MIKE BOYLE

288 Palisade Avenue • Jersey City, New Jersey 07306 • 201-555-2938

JOB DESIRED   Apprentice mechanic with automotive repair company with opportunity to train as auto mechanic.

EDUCATION   Dickinson High School, Jersey City, 1990 to present

Hudson Regional Junior-Senior High School, Highlands, NJ, 1988-90

SKILLS
- Mechanically inclined, with skills ranging from basic auto mechanics to very technical electrical diagnostics.
- Experienced with engine overhaul, suspension, brakes, fuel, and power train.
- Experienced with motor detailing.
- Some auto-body repair experience.

WORK EXPERIENCE   <u>Dickinson High School Auto Shop</u>, 1991-present

- Duties include: Tune-ups, oil changes, general check-up and trouble shooting in student-run auto mechanics shop. Diagnose and repair mechanical problems on cars, trucks, and vans.

<u>East Jersey Radiator</u>, 1991-present

- Duties include: Cleaning and testing radiators, installing replacement radiators, and motor detailing. Shop services both foreign and domestic cars. Assisted with stock warehouse.

<u>Northern Landscape Maintenance</u>, 1990-1991

- Duties included: Planting, mowing, pruning, and hedging for three apartment complexes and four office complexes. Responsible for maintaining nursery inventory.

REFERENCES   Available upon request

ARLENE HOSAKA

2833 Kennedy Boulevard
Jersey City, New Jersey 07305

Telephone: (201) 555-5198
Message: (201) 555-9877

OBJECTIVE

To obtain a position as receptionist for a law office, with a long-range goal of training for advancement to a position as legal secretary.

EDUCATION

1988 - 92

St. Aloysius High School
721 West Side Avenue
Jersey City, NJ 07306
Expected graduation date: 1992

Courses of study: business law, typing, computer applications, marketing I, accounting I, Japanese II. Current G.P.A.: 3.6

1992 -

Drake Secretarial College
905 Bergen Avenue
Jersey City, NJ 07306

Currently enrolled in shorthand dictation and standard business systems.

WORK EXPERIENCE

6/91 - 8/91

Receptionist at Law Office of Dupuy, Jakewith, Howard & Taft
Worked as summer replacement receptionist. Responsible for operating telephone switchboard for an office of eight attorneys, six legal assistants, five legal secretaries, and three law clerks. Organized computer mail software installation on all office computers. Typed legal documents as needed.

9/89 - 6/91

Student Office Assistant, St. Aloysius High School
Worked in the High School office, answered telephones, greeted visitors, and assisted school secretaries as needed with filing and typing. Responsible for maintaining daily attendance records for distribution to teachers.

SKILLS

Ability to operate the following: check register, word processor, dictaphone, and adding machine.

ACTIVITIES

Future Business Leaders of America, Marketing Club, National Honor Society, and one year of tennis

REFERENCES

Available on request

JORDAN WILEY
Rural Route 31, Box 243
Cicero, New York 13039
(315) 555-2446

JOB OBJECTIVE

Retail sales position with local merchant.

EDUCATION

Cicero-North Syracuse Senior High School
Rural Route 31, Cicero, NY 13039
Expected graduation date: 1993

> *Related Courses:* Accounting I and II, Business Systems, Math (through Algebra II),
> Computer Operations

Student Training Education Program (STEP)
1421 Stark Street, Syracuse, NY 13039

> *Related Courses:* Personal Finance

WORK HISTORY

Chums Cafe, 1/5/90 - 6/25/91
204 NE Second, Syracuse, New York
Supervisor: Ike Jung

Little Caesar Restaurant, 7/12/89 - 1/2/90
1835 NE Division, Syracuse, New York
Supervisor: Sandra Pommerville

ACTIVITIES

Offices Held	Secretary, Future Business Leaders of America, 1991; President, Bike & Hike Club, 1990-1991
Committees	Homecoming, 1991 - 1992; Junior & Senior Prom Committee, 1990 - 1991
Memberships	Cub Scouts 1980 - 1984; Bike & Hike Club, 1989 - 1992; Youth Convention, 1989, 1990, 1991; Syracuse Swiss Sportsman Club, 1978 - 1990
Sports	Football, 1987 - 1991; Indoor Track, 1991 - 1992
Hobbies	Traveling, cycling, skiing, collecting baseball and basketball cards, hiking

References available on request

DAVID JAKES
2390 N. Harvey, No. 1
Baltimore, Maryland 21225
(503) 555-6870

OBJECTIVE

Obtain an entry-level position in a business where my organizational and leadership skills can help make a positive difference.

EDUCATION

- Douglass High School
Expected graduation date June 1994

RELATED COURSEWORK

Personal Finance, Career Education, Marketing, Computer Keyboarding.
Current GPA: 3.28

EXPERIENCE & SKILLS DEVELOPMENT

- Promote sales of martial arts merchandise and karate lessons.
- Assist with office operations, answer telephones, schedule lesson times, assist students and clients.
- Teach Kenpo Karate, Thai Boxing, and Freestyle Sparring to children and adults, in both private and group class situations.
- Distribute flyers to individuals on college campuses and in mall parking lots.
- Abilities include: sales, telephone communications, computer keyboarding, organization, and customer service.

WORK HISTORY

Baltimore Kenpo Karate School, August 1991-present

ACTIVITIES

Karate and karate tournaments, swimming, mountain climbing, reading, cycling, basketball, music.

REFERENCES

Available on request.

Alicia Bernard
3180 SE Pelton Avenue
Rumford, Maine 04276   (207) 555-0590

Objective	Secretarial or receptionist position.

Education

1989 - present	Mountain Valley High School, Hancock Street, Rumford, ME
	Relevant courses: Keyboarding, Office Systems, Personal Finance, Russian; currently enrolled in Shorthand.
Spring 1988	Anna Falaci's Charm School, Mountain Road, Oxford, ME

Work Experience

July - Aug. 1992	Landscaping, Crest Landscaping Services My responsibilities included pruning, trimming, weeding, and mowing for a variety of business and individual clients.
June - Aug. 1991	Assistant, Duckworth Boats My duties included working with the public, serving as receptionist, typing, answering telephones, bookkeeping, filing, receiving and sending shipments. Also washed and detailed boats and assisted at boat shows.
June-Aug. 1990	Volunteer, Animal Services, Oxford County Animal Control I was responsible for feeding and bathing animals in the animal control shelter, showing pets to prospective owners, and answering telephones.
1986 - present	Child Care Provider, various individuals. Providing childcare to children ages 6 weeks to 9 years, from one to three children at a time.
1986 - 1989	General Assistant, Webb's K.E. Carlson Co. Duties included: filing, typing, computer operations, cleaning, running errands.

Skills

Computer keyboarding, communications and telephone skills, filing, general office work.

References	Available on request.

Kim Gravenstein
111 N.E. 92nd
Lexington, Kentucky 40503
(606) 555-4900

Job Objective   *Part-time secretarial support services.*

Education

1988 - 1992   Bryan Station Senior High School

                    Courses of study:
                    keyboarding I and II
                    office systems
                    two years of business

Work History

1989 - present   *Child Care Provider*
                    Rock Creek Lanes, Lexington

                    Duties: provide quality childcare in playroom and maintain records
                    and billing for childcare.

1987 - 1989   *Child Care Provider*
                    Private Individuals

                    Provided full-time summer care for two children in a private home
                    and frequent intermittent evening and weekend care.

Office Skills   Ability to operate the following: computer word processing
                    (75 wpm, IBM Word Perfect), ten-key adding machine, and
                    typewriter (50 wpm).

Activities   4-H horse section, Junior Rodeo, two years of team polo.

References   Available on request.

Jackson Garvey
1133 N.E. 14th
El Dorado, Kansas 67042
(316) 555-3086

Career Goal

My short-term objective is to obtain a position as a warehouseman. For the long-term, my goal is to complete college training in engineering and manufacturing.

Education

El Dorado High School, McCullom Road, El Dorado

Courses studied: metal shop, computer applications, three years of woodworking, and three-dimensional design.

Work Experience

Warehouse Worker, Gates Tire Company, El Dorado, Kansas, *June to August 1992.*
   Assisted with receiving shipments, stocking, and sending shipments. Drove forklift and operated loading dock.

Landscape Maintenance for private individuals. *June to August 1991.*
   Planted and removed plants and provided lawn maintenance for a variety of personal clients.

Field Worker, Townsend Farms, Inc., *June to August 1990*
   Planting and harvesting for several crops for small family farm operation.

Skills

Able to operate the following: lathe, table saw, drill press, sander, bench grinder, arc welder, loading dock, Hyster 2450 forklift.

Activities

Junior varsity and varsity baseball and soccer. Member of Greater El Dorado Soccer Club.

References

Available on request.

Shelley Tabor

78 N.E. Towbridge
Bridgewater, Massachusetts 02324
(508) 555-8281

Objective

Assistant's position with preschool or child care facility.

Education

Bridgewater-Raynham Regional High School, Mt. Prospect Street.
Expected graduation date 1993.

Specialized Courses: Early Childhood Development, Childhood
Education/Preschool, Human Development, Preschool Practicum (hands-on
experience at the day care/preschool), Health and First Aid.

Relevant Work Experience

1987-present
Childcare provider for various private individuals. For two summers, provided full-
time care for three children, ages 18 months to 6 years.

1991-present
Supervisor and Assistant, Girl Scout Troop #475. Help to organize and plan
activities. Coached troop softball team summer of 1992.

1991-1992
Group Leader, 4-H, Sheep Division. Worked with group of six 5th and 6th grade
students to raise Hampshire sheep. Sponsored sheep at state fair in Springfield.

References

Available on request.

Jennifer Hartshore

17327 N.E. Waterton • Boston, Massachusetts 02215 • 617-555-2239

Job Desired

Part-time secretarial position.

Education

September 1992 - present
Wheelock College, 200 Riverway, Boston

Course of study: Business management, accounting, finance.

1987 - 1992
Cathedral High School, 74 Union Park Street, Boston

Courses taken: typing II, office systems and procedures, marketing I, computer applications; currently enrolled in Spanish IV, accounting II, and business law.

August - October 1989
Academy One Modeling Course

Work Experience

September 1990 - present
Typist at Opti-Craft Laboratory, Inc., Boston

June - August 1989 and 1990
Secretarial Assistant at Barker Enterprises, Inc.

August 1988 - July 1999
Attendant at Bruce & Bill's Arco Station.

Skills

Ability to operate the following: cash register, ten-key adding machine, IBM computer (Works word processing software, 70 wpm), typewriter (55 wpm), and dictaphone.

Activities

Future Business Leaders of America, National Honor Society, one year of team volleyball.

References   Available on request.

JANINE HARTNEY
16825 N.E. Clarkston
Battle Creek, Michigan 49017
Telephone: 616-555-3420

JOB SOUGHT   Position in retail sales for hardware or electronic products.

EDUCATION

1989 - 1993
Battle Creek Central Senior High School, Battle Creek, Michigan

Specialized coursework:
marketing I
Spanish IV
accounting II
electronics
woodworking shop

WORK EXPERIENCE

11/91 - present
Battle Creek Auto Parts
Duties include: serving customers, maintaining warehouse supply, stocking and shelving parts, receiving shipments. (Left when store closed.)

2/90 - 10/91
Wendy's Store #1023.
Duties included: fast food preparation, order processing, clean-up and operation of kitchen machinery.

ACTIVITIES

Outdoor school counselor, one year of basketball. Hobbies include electronics, model building, basketball, volleyball, football, bicycling, and tennis.

REFERENCES   Available on request

• **Juan Aguilar** •

158 Halladay S.W.
Benton Harbor, Michigan 49028

Telephone: 616-555-7379

• **Job Desired** •

Printer's apprentice in newspaper printing department.

• **Education** •

1989 - present
Benton Harbor High School; Expected graduation date: June 1993.

• Pertinent courses: graphic arts, journalism, photography, typing II, word processing.

• **Skills & Experience** •

Ability to operate the following: Graphic printing press, screen printer, camera, copy machine, Compugraphic 2824 typesetter, Macintosh computer (Quark Xpress, PageMaker, Adobe Photoshop, Aldus Freehand).

• **Work Experience** •

Printing assistant for Michigan Printing. Summer 1992.

Assisted with preparing camera-ready mechanicals for film, making photo negatives for printing plates, positioning plates on press, checking press runs, operating cutter and folder. Worked with stripping department on cutting masks and windows in film.

Production chief for Harbor High Herald. 1991-present.

Duties include set-up and layout of boards for printing preparation. Have recently begun transfer from traditional typesetting and layout to electronic pre-press with ability to scan photographs into system, then crop and size electronically to fit layout of text and other graphics.

House painting for private residences, interior and exterior. Summers of 1990 and 1991.

• **References** •

Available on request

WENDY SWANSON
1602 Newport Road
Ann Arbor, Michigan 48105
(313) 555-0226

JOB OBJECTIVE

Lab assistant with opportunities to apply computers in scientific problem-solving.

EDUCATION

1989 - present
Clague High School, 2616 Nixon Road, Ann Arbor, Michigan
Expected graduation date: June 1993

> *Coursework:* three years of science (chemistry, physics, biology), three years of math (through pre-calculus), and computer applications in science.

SKILLS

My experience in the student science laboratory has given me the background required to be valuable to a scientific research effort. I am able to follow instructions with scientific precision and record data for further analysis. I have operated a wide range of scientific equipment and done independent projects involving dissection, blood tests and analysis, and computer sampling.

WORK HISTORY

August 1991 to present
Teacher's assistant, Clague High School, Mr. Jay Bradmoore
> *Duties include:* Working with students in science classes to perform lab experiments; helping teachers pass out lab materials; scoring lab work sheets.

October 1990 to July 1991
Courtesy Clerk, Art's Glisan Thriftway
> *Duties included:* Serving customers by packaging and delivering groceries to their parked cars, stocking, providing additional assistance as needed.

June to August 1990
Childcare provider, private home

ACTIVITIES

Vice President of Science Club; active in Odyssey of the Mind; involved in choir; enjoy singing, reading, and traveling.

REFERENCES available upon request.

✦ Stephanie Volk ✦
1340 North Park Drive
St. Paul, Minnesota 55106
(612) 555-9851

✦ OBJECTIVE   Retail sales position in fashion boutique or department store.

✦ EDUCATION

1989 - present: Johnson High School, St. Paul.

✦ one year computers
✦ one year typing
✦ one year accounting

✦ one year teacher assistant
✦ two years business systems
✦ one semester personal finance

✦ WORK EXPERIENCE

September 1991 - present: Store Manager, Johnson High Hut
Supervise and schedule student workers in high school student store. Maintain stock
and order merchandise from several different vendors. Work with teacher/advisor on
budget and bookkeeping. Conducted student survey to determine interests and
varied merchandise accordingly. Organized marketing campaign that increased sales
by 20 percent in a single month.

June 1990 - August 1991: Line clerk, Taco Haven
Served customers, prepared and checked food orders, handled money, balanced
cash drawer at end of shift, and helped open and close the restaurant.

July 1991: Volunteer, Twin Cities Women's Softball Association
Maintained score sheet for annual softball playoffs.

June 1990: Volunteer, Minneapolis Metro Softball Association
Maintained score sheet for Men's 40 and Over National Tournament.

✦ SKILLS

Experienced with operating cash registers, computers, ten-key adding machine;
typing rate of 65 wpm; work well with people.

✦ ACTIVITIES

Future Business Leaders of America, student business club (store manager),
freshman volleyball, junior basketball, freshman and junior softball.

✦ REFERENCES are available on request.

♦ Michelle M. Hibbard
3320 Delaware Avenue
Erie, New York 14222
(716) 555-2193

♦ **Education**

1989 - present: Marshfield Girls Academy, 24 Shoshone Street, Erie, New York

1981 - present: Private voice lessons; Roseanne Valdivieso and Pauline Jenson, Erie

1979-1985: Judy Andresch School of Dance, Erie

♦ **Experience**

1991 - present: der Rheinlander Restaurant, Academy Boulevard, Erie
Singing Hostess. Responsibilities include greeting and seating customers and
providing musical entertainment.

1991 - present: Balloons, Etc., West McKinley Parkway, Erie
Delivery person. Responsibilities include driving company van to deliver balloon
bouquets, flowers, and singing telegrams.

1988 - present: Providing child care in private homes
Duties include caring for four children ages 2 to 7, providing meals and first aid.

1985 - present: Singing in weddings and at private entertainments

♦ **Achievements**

First soloist for the Erie County Youth Choir, 1991 and 1992
Marshfield Girls Choir
Marshfield Dance Team, Captain
Youth of the Month, Erie Elks Lodge No. 125, January 1991
Junior Class President, 1991
National Honor Society Scholar of the Year, 1992
State letter in girl's volleyball
Speak conversational German

♦ **References**

Available upon request

Brandon Smith

317 W. Trinity, Apt. 6
Durham, North Carolina 27708

Telephone: 555-2930

Education

Hillside High School, 1900 Concord Street, Durham
Expected graduation date: 1993

Durham Technical Community College, Special Summer Session
Attended Summer 1992, pre-engineering

Relevant Training

Three years of Math (through Trigonometry), Practical Physics, Chemistry, Woods II, Metals II, and Building Construction.

Experience and Skills

Assisted with framing and roofing two new houses. Completed roof repair project on cedar-shake roof. Removed and replaced siding on one wall of shingle-sided house.

Provided landscape maintenance for private homes, including lawn mowing, weeding, trimming, hedging, and some planting.

Through school course work I have developed the ability to operate a lathe, table saw, drill press, and other metal and woodworking machinery, as well as typewriter, IBM computer (word processing and DISCOVER software), and HP 95X scientific calculator.

Work Record

John Jalletty Construction, 421 Driver Street, Durham; June-August 1991

Hillside High School, Wood Shop Assistant, Durham; September 1991-June 1992

Activities

Baseball, football, and track teams. Hobbies include snow boarding, body boarding, bicycling, traveling, and building models.

References

Available upon request.

GARRY LUPAS
809 N. Washington Street
Bismarck, North Dakota 58501
Telephone: 555-3994

OBJECTIVE

Position in agri-business utilizing my supervisory and organizational skills.

EDUCATION

Central Senior High School, 1000 East Century Avenue, Bismarck
  Diploma awarded 1992

  Courses completed: business series courses in agriculture, law, and marketing; special project course in which I devised and prepared a marketing and development plan for a new agricultural support services business.

RELEVANT EXPERIENCE

Hay Bailer/Field Boss, Klair & Klock Larson Farm. Summers of 1989, 1990, & 1991
  Worked each summer in berry fields, earning at the top 10 percent of all field hands (paid by tons bailed). In 1991, I was hired as a field boss and was responsible for supervising workers, paying fees, and checking for quality.

Swim Instructor/Life Guard, Bismarck Community Pool. 9/90-6/91
  Supervised swim activities at indoor pool facility. Taught swimming lessons to 4th, 5th, and 6th grade children. Hold current life saving certificate.

SKILLS & ACTIVITIES

  Experienced with wide range of farm implements and machinery. Hold valid driver's license. Swim team (first place in state competition).

REFERENCES

Available on request.

ERIN R. DURANT
223 Brittain Road
Redmond, Washington 98052
(206) 555-3380

EDUCATION

Redmond Senior High School: Expected graduation date: 1992

Specialized Courses: Home building construction, PGE Good Sense Home; Wood Shop; Auto Technology. (4.0 GPA in these areas)

SKILLS

As a result of both regular and freelance employment, I have gained specific job-related skills in the following areas: logging, wood cutting, pipe laying, heavy equipment operation, carpentry, general house repair and maintenance, yard work, house painting, automotive repair.

WORK EXPERIENCE

Laborer for Mike Jensen, September 1991 to present.
Stripped and replumbed a bathroom; cleaned gutters, installed insulation; removed shrubbery.

Laborer for Scott Farris (Private Contractor), eight months in 1990 and 1991.
Completed deck repairs, washed and painted buildings, trimmed trees, shored up a retaining wall. Also involved with roof repair, window cleaning, car repair, and moving and transportation.

Laborer for Wolcott Excavating, summers of 1990 and 1991.
Worked on ditch digging, ran errands in company truck to obtain pipe and blueprints, made deliveries of pipe and fixtures, read blueprints, installed insulation, took inventory, filled orders, organized stock. Operated chain saw, jumping jack, 580K backhoe, Halton cat loader, Halton cat D4, Case 24-ton roller, and drove dump truck.

I have also worked on several other short-term contractor jobs doing carpentry and general labor.

ACTIVITIES

Four years wrestling letterman, two years football, track official for the track teams, student government, and building construction and wood shop.

References are available upon request.

STEPHANIE TIRRELL
889 Copley Road
Akron, Ohio 44308
Telephone: (216) 555-1941

OBJECTIVE

Because of my love for children and my interest in their development, I am seeking a position as a caregiver in a quality preschool or day care environment.

EDUCATION

Central Hower High School, 123 N. Forge Street, Akron, Ohio 44304
  Expected graduation date: 1993
  Specialized courses: Child Development, Early Childhood Education.

Mt. Union College, 1972 Clark Avenue, Akron, Ohio 44601
  Summer of 1992 open enrollment program.
  Courses: Child Development, Beginning Psychology

RELATED EXPERIENCE

Childcare: I have been providing competent childcare since 1987. I provide care consistently for four children in two different families.

Counseling: In October 1990 and April 1991, I worked as a counselor at the Trout Creek Outdoor School, supervising sixth grade students and teaching basic plant identification and plant ecology. Also presented lessons on plants at several grade schools.

Volunteer: Since June 1990 I have offered tours at the Akron Park Zoo, educating children about zoo animals, natural habitat, and endangered species. During October 1991 I participated in the "Zoo Boo" Train. I dressed in costume and entertained train riders along the route.

REFERENCES

Available on request.

Aisha Mgazi
289 Windvale Drive
Pittsburgh, Pennsylvania 15236
Telephone: (412) 555-9027

Job Desired

Sales clerk or customer service representative for major department store.

Education

Baldwin High School, 4653 Clairton Boulevard, Pittsburgh
Graduation date: June, 1993

Work Experience

Courtesy Clerk, A&G Food Centers, 181st & Parkfield, April 1990 - present.
My primary responsibility is to assist customers in locating items and taking purchases to their cars. I also bag groceries, count bottles, stock shelves, and provide additional assistance as needed.

Assistant, Monograms Plus, City Center Mall, Summer 1989 & Nov. 1989 - Jan. 1990.
Responsible for monogramming shirts, sweatshirts, shorts, and jackets; providing customer service; and stocking shelves.

Sales Representative, Accents, City Center Mall, November 1988 to January 1989.
Served customers, coordinated sales, operated the cash register, and assisted with maintaining stock.

Skills

Accurately operate a cash register and handle cash and credit card financial transfers. Experienced with IBM-compatible computer word processing software and can type 70 words per minute (60 wpm on electric typewriter).

Activities

Served as a counselor at Outdoor School, am a member of International Club and Multicultural Students Organization, have played three years of team volleyball, and work at school track meets.

References

Available upon request.

Raymond Koller
P. O. Box 229
Elk City, Oklahoma 73644
Telephone: (405) 555-1665

Objective
Reporter position on weekly newspaper

Skills
* Accurate and reliable reporting skills
* Trained in black-and-white photography (own equipment & several lenses)
* Experienced in developing and printing black-and-white film
* Skilled with word processing and page layout software on Macintosh
* Experienced with newspaper layout and production procedures

Education
Elk City Senior High School, 222 W. Broadway
Graduation date: 1992

During high school my course work focused on writing, government, history, journalism, and photography in preparation for a career in journalism.

Work Experience

Elk City Daily News, 200-206 W. Broadway. 1986-1990.
Duties: Published two articles in August 1991 and January 1992. During the summers of 1990 to 1992 I worked in the news editorial section of the newspaper, where I compiled newspaper index records, researched prior articles for reporters and editors, and provided general assistance. I also delivered the daily newspaper and collected monthly fees throughout the year.

Elk City High Gazette, Senior Editor. 1991-1992.
Duties: Assigned stories to student reporters, interviewed faculty and students and wrote articles for quarterly student publication, determined layout of newspaper, assisted with production and layout of newspaper on Macintosh computer, shot and developed photographs for publication. Worked as reporter 1990-1991.

References and portfolio of photography and published articles available on request.

Andrew Linden
1182 Howard Avenue
Altoona, Pennsylvania 16602
Telephone: (814) 555-7367

OBJECTIVE

Computer technician position that will take advantage of my background in computer languages and programming.

ACCOMPLISHMENTS

o Selected as Senior Lab Assistant for the school computer lab
o Supervised and assisted students during computer classes and open lab sessions
o Created program in BASIC for a math tutorial
o Created program in COBOL for random number processing
o Assisted teacher in development of computer lab manuals
o Completed college-level computer courses while in high school, receiving top grades

EDUCATION

Altoona Senior High School
Diploma awarded: 1992. GPA: 3.93.

Computer Learning Network
Summer programs, 1990 and 1991

Courses of study: Computer programming, COBOL, BASIC, PASCAL, math (three years, through honors college algebra and trigonometry), Japanese I and II.

WORK HISTORY

Software module worker, Noreast Publishing, Altoona. June 1991-present.
  Duties: Perform data entry using word processing and spreadsheet software.

Altoona High School, Computer Lab. 1989-1992.
  Duties: Assisted as student volunteer. Worked with students during lab sessions. Answered questions. Assisted in development of lab manuals. Developed working knowledge of all software available in the lab.

Pizza Haven, Altoona, Don Swingen, supervisor. Summer 1990.

REFERENCES   Available on request.

• **Brian Schlosser** •
243 Mount Pleasant Avenue • Providence, Rhode Island 02903 • 401/555-2335

Objective

- To obtain part-time employment as a stage hand for theatrical productions in a small theatrical company.

Education

- Hope High School. Will graduate in June 1993. Current GPA: 3.3.

- Shea High School, Pawtucket, Rhode Island. Attended 1990-1991.

Relevant Experience

- Worked as stage manager for three school productions
- Operated lights and sound for musical production of "Oklahoma"
- Assisted with set design and building for three plays
- Experienced with all aspects of theatrical production
- Worked as stage hand for a production at Brown University
- Played the lead in "Brigadoon"
- Sang in the chorus in "Godspell"

Work History

- Cashier and line cook for Taco Time, Providence. 4/89-present.

- Paper distributor for the Pawtucket Evening News. 3/87-3/89.

Activities

- Member of Thespian Society. Participated in various aspects of student theatrical productions at Hope High School.

- Madrigal Singers and Concert Choir, Shea High School.

References

- Available on request.

Dañela Murar
810 Fifth Street N.
Canton, South Dakota 57013
(605) 555-9530

Objective

Entry-level position with an international corporation where my bilingual skills may make a contribution to the organization.

Education

- Canton High School, 112 Elder Avenue E., Canton, SD 57013
  Graduation date: 1992.

- Magnolia High School, 2540 W. Ball Road, Anaheim, CA 92804.
  Attended 1988-1990.

- Attended school in Romania during 1990-91 school year.

Training

- Computer applications experience: Word on IBM and Mac;
  Lotus 1-2-3, dBase, and Harvard Graphics on IBM.

- Typing (55 wpm on typewriter; 70 on computer word processor)

- Office systems course covered bookkeeping, filing, telephone switchboards, personnel and payroll.

- Gregg shorthand (115 wpm)

- Fluent in Spanish; conversant in Romanian.

Work Experience

- Attendance office assistant, Canton Senior High School, Sept. 1991-present
  Duties: answer telephones, assist students and faculty, prepare daily announcements list on computer, operate office machines, type and file.

- Cashier, Kentucky Fried Chicken, June 1991-Sept. 1991
  Duties: Completed customer orders, entered sales in cash register, provided accurate change.

- Cashier, McDonald's, Anaheim, CA, July 1989-Aug. 1990
  Duties: Completed customer orders, entered sales in cash register, provided accurate change; general assistance as needed.

References

- Available on request

LEVARR JOHNSON
2234 Cunningham Lane
Clarksville, Tennessee 37042
(615) 555-8117

JOB SOUGHT

Entry level electronics technician.

EDUCATION

Northwest High School, Lafayette Road, Clarksville
Diploma awarded June 1992. Grade point average: 3.87
Major: Technology and Electronics

Civil Air Patrol (U.S. Air Force Auxiliary), 1989 to present.

SKILLS

Trained in electronics repair at Civil Air Patrol (oscilloscopes, radios, radar)

Completed two years in technology and electronics courses at Northwest High

Repaired disassembled television set to working order

Experienced in operating compression tools for construction

WORK HISTORY

Construction Worker for Johnson Construction, April 1988 to present.

Major duties: Framed and roofed homes, hauled lumber to job site in company truck, checked lumber delivery against purchase order.

Pizza Chef at Little Caesar's, Clarksville, Tennessee

REFERENCES

Available on request

Brian McGavin
990 Woody Road
Dallas, Texas 75253
(214) 555-2369

OBJECTIVE
A career in business management. Immediate goal is an entry-level position with a growing business.

EDUCATION
- Lake Highlands Senior High School. Graduation: May 1992
  Specialized Courses:
  - Business I & II
  - Computer Science (two years)
  - Spanish I & II
  - Current GPA: 3.0

EXPERIENCE
- Assistant Manager, Taco Bell Restaurant, May 1991 to present. Started as line cook, June 1989; promoted to cashier, November 1989; promoted to assistant manager with supervisory responsibility May 1991.

- Assistant Manager, Student Store, Lake Highlands Senior High, September 1989 to June 1990. Responsible for scheduling workers for student store operation. Checked accuracy of cash reports and tracked any discrepancies. Assisted manager with ordering stock and receiving shipments.

- Student Assistant, Counseling Office, Lake Highlands Senior High, September 1988 to June 1989. Worked for four counselors, answered telephones, scheduled appointments, typed letters. Student assistants were selected on the basis of ability, skills, and trustworthiness.

ACTIVITIES
- Future Business Leaders of America
- DECA (Diversified Education Clubs of America, a marketing club)
- Attended Texas Business Week at American Institute of Commerce, Dallas, Texas
- Currently Vice President of DECA, which operates the student store at Lake Highlands Senior High School.

REFERENCES Available on request.

Tamany Pryde
2339 S.E. Kibling Avenue
Tyler, Texas 75710
(214) 555-0422

Job Sought

Summer internship in graphic design that will utilize my computer drawing and layout skills and provide opportunities for further training.

Education

Lee High School. Anticipated graduation date: May 1993
- art and graphics (three years)
- computer applications
- computer programming
- drafting/mechanical drawing
- current GPA: 3.29

Work Experience

Graphic Artist, student publications (newspaper, yearbook)
- Designed logos and mastheads.
- Established design formats for entire newspaper.
- Worked with design and production team to design yearbook.
- Designed yearbook cover.
- Set up computer templates on Macintosh using Publish-It Easy.
- Worked with editors on layout of each issue of the newspaper.
- Designed advertisements for student clubs for both publications.
- Created new computer clip art and altered existing art, using Claris MacPaint and MacDraw programs.

References are available on request.

Sherrita Gonzalez

235 Gramercy Avenue
Ogden, Utah 84404
(801) 555-1409

Objective

Obtain a summer internship with a local business so that I may utilize my clerical skills and learn more about personnel issues. My long-term goal is a career in personnel management.

Education

Lomond High School, Ogden   Class of 1994

Courses pertinent to job objective: business and economics, computer applications, typing, career education. GPA: 3.28.
Currently serving as a counseling office assistant, where I answer telephones, type, file, and schedule appointments.

Work Experience

Wimpy's Burgers, 560 N.W. Phoenix Drive, Ogden   1991 to present
Responsibilities: serve customers, prepare food, operate cash register, handle money, close store.

Jazzercise, 2466 E. Burns, Ogden   1991 to present
Responsibilities: provide quality care for children of parents participating in Jazzercise exercise programs.

Skills

I am experienced with Macintosh and IBM computers, and I have good typing (70 wpm), filing, and telephone communications skills. I am also a quick learner and strive to be accurate in everything I do. Fluent Spanish speaker.

References

Available on request.

Kendra Wallen

1137 N.E. 189th • Provo, Utah 84604 • (801) 555-2740

Objective

Student teaching for summer art camp programs.

Education

Timpview High School, class of 1993
Courses include: childhood education, art (two years), advanced studio painting, and computer applications in art.

Experience

Since June of 1988, I have worked as a child care provider to children of various ages, responsible for preparing food, feeding, diapering, and general care. Each summer I worked full-time and offered innovative children's art projects that were designed for specific ages and abilities.

In June of 1990 and 1991 I taught art during vacation Bible school program for elementary school children on the Navajo Reservation.

Special Skills

Ability to operate a variety of computer software and hardware programs, specifically programs providing graphic arts and page layout capabilities. Hold valid CPR card.

References and portfolio of children's projects are available on request.

15 Church Street
Rutland, Vermont 05701
(802) 555-1939

Aki Mioshi

Job Sought
> Department store security staff position, working evenings or weekends.

Education

<u>Rutland High School</u>, 67 Library Avenue, Rutland
> Class of 1993
> Current GPA: 3.7

<u>State Police Explorer Program</u>
> Attended: Summer 1989

Accomplishments

• Started RADD, Rutlanders Against Drugs and Drinking
• Elected Vice President of Junior Class, Rutland High School
• Lettered in track and field, volleyball, and softball
• Listed on Honor Roll every semester since Freshman year
• Fluent in spoken Japanese

Work History

<u>Waitress: The Pines Restaurant</u>, Rutland   10/91 - present
> Duties: greet and serve customers, communicate orders to kitchen staff, direct preparation of salads and desserts. Responsible for quality of service provided to customers. Earned bonus for excellence and courtesy, December 1991.

References are available on request.

v i n q u a m p h o n g

1321 Longview Drive ▼ Woodbridge, Virginia 22192 ▼ 703-555-4958

▼ o b j e c t i v e

Entry-level graphic arts or production position.

▼ e x p e r i e n c e

Gar-Field News
Production Chief, 1991-1992
Graphic Artist, 1990-1991

Created layout for student newspaper. Designed advertisements. Prepared paste-up boards for printing. Sized and cropped photographs for reproduction. Specified type sizes and styles for typesetters. Selected and designed art images to enhance visual design of newspaper. Worked with editorial staff to determine placement of news articles and photographs.

Free-lance Artist
1990-present

Designed and prepared mechanicals of logo for my father's restaurant supply business. Drew portraits at State Fair. Worked for several student groups to design banners, signs and logos for school-related activities.

▼ e d u c a t i o n

Gar-Field High School. Anticipated date of graduation: 1993

My elective course work has focused on art and design, often involving extra-curricular projects because I had completed the class assignments and sought additional opportunities to challenge my skills. Art and Design GPA: 4.0.

▼ r e f e r e n c e s

Available on request.

JASON RAINTREE
2268-A S. 187th Street
Seattle, Washington 98055
(206) 555-9225

OBJECTIVE   Summer internship with social service agency

EDUCATION

Tyee High School, 4224 S. 188th Street, Seattle
Graduation Class of 1992
Cumulative Grade Point Average: 3.47

Course work designed to provide broad background with some specific training in areas useful to social services, including:

* child development
* sociology
* psychology
* writing for business
* U.S. government
* Spanish (three years)

EXPERIENCE & ACHIEVEMENTS

Volunteer assistant at Boys and Girls Club of South Seattle. Coached and refereed elementary school children on sports teams in basketball, soccer, and softball. Helped counselors with "Just Say No" educational programs.

Coordinated, with three other students, an anti-drug club that sponsored alcohol and drug-free events and activities as well as an annual drug awareness assembly. Our goal was to increase the status of being drug-free. In the first year, we had 50 percent participation throughout the school.

Selected by South Seattle Rotary Club International to present an essay celebrating Seattle's Native American heritage and proposing some remedies for the problems facing Native Americans in today's society.

REFERENCES are available on request.

Robert Goldstein
2250 Collis Avenue
Huntington, West Virginia 25702
Telephone: 304-555-9941

Job Sought   Training position with Huntington Fire District.

Education   Cabel County Vocational-Technical Senior High
                   Diploma, Class of 1992.

                   Major: Health and Physical Education. Courses
                   included: health and human fitness, human anatomy,
                   safety and first aid, human development.

Experience   Referee, West Hills Soccer Club, 1988-present
                   Work during summers and on weekends to referee soccer
                   games and tournaments for elementary and junior high
                   school level soccer teams.

                   Referee and Ticket Sales, CCVTSHS, 1988-90
                   Served as practice referee during basketball team
                   practice sessions. Sold tickets at entrance for home
                   basketball games.

                   Trained in CPR and advanced life saving.

                   Trained in gun safety.

Activities &
Awards   President's Council on Physical Fitness, first award

                   Varsity football, letter award

                   Varsity track and field, letter award

References   Available on request.

```
Anjala Hindagolla
2325 Rapids Drive
Racine, Wisconsin 53406
(414) 555-8733
```

Objective   Cook or chef's assistant in Middle Eastern restaurant.

Experience   <u>Ramdalla</u>, Milwaukee, Wisconsin, 1988-1990

* Worked in former family restaurant as chef's
  assistant.
* Operated kitchen machinery.
* Prepared foods from recipes.
* Maintained oven and grill cleanliness.
* Prepared serving plates for beautiful visual
  presentation.
* Gained experience in all aspects of restaurant food
  preparation.

Education   <u>Case High School</u>, Racine, Wisconsin, Class of 1993

Specialized courses:
* home economics I and II
* food science and nutrition
* business operations
* food preparation and safety (special workshop at state
  health division)

References   Available on request.

Darryl J. Richmond
356 N. Alameda
Santa Rosa, California 95406
(707) 555-3964

Objective   Summer carpenter crew position with home construction company.

Experience

Tiara Construction Co.
5316 S.E. Francis, Sebastapol, California 95472
Summer 1990 and 1991
Supervisor: George Linde, (707) 776-5015

Worked with carpentry crew; framed and roofed houses; sheetrocked interiors; installed insulation in walls and rafters.

Growers Outlet, Stocker.
15165 S.E. Laguna Blvd., Santa Rosa, California 95403
September 1990 to present
Supervisor: Janet Brendler, (707) 844-2000

Work with grocery supervisor to stock shelves, receive and direct shipments of produce, maintain quality presentation in produce department.

Education

Santa Rosa High School
2156 Cerritos, Santa Rosa, California 95401
Expected graduation date: 1993

Pertinent courses: wood and metal shop, building construction, mechanical drawing, architecture.

Santa Rosa Middle School
1800 Terra Blvd., Santa Rosa, California 95401

Pertinent courses: wood shop.

References

Available on request.

Janice Anne Richland
10205 Catlin Avenue
Brookline, Massachusetts 02146
(617) 555-0116

Objective

Retail sales position with music-related store.

Skills

Good knowledge of both contemporary and classical music. Work well with people. Ability to operate cash registers and most office equipment.

Work Experience

Cashier   Wendy's Hamburger Restaurant, Thayer Road, Brookline
Supervisor: Raejean Matthews (617) 255-9444
June 1991 to present

Duties   Greet customers, take orders, communicate orders to line cooks, operate cash register, handle cash, close and balance register receipts at shift's end.

Clerical
Assistant   Brookline High School, Senior Office
Supervisor: Annette Jameson (617) 215-7800
Summer 1990

Duties   Answer telephones, route calls through six-line switchboard, type letters, file, greet visitors, assist students and teachers as needed.

Education

Brookline High School, Brookline, Massachusetts
Expected graduation date: 1993
Pertinent Courses: Wind ensemble, orchestra, jazz band, choir, music theory, business.

Standish Middle School, Boston, Massachusetts
September 1988 - June 1990
Pertinent Courses: Concert band, jazz band.

Achievements

First place league solo 1992; four Outstanding Solo Jazz awards 1991-92; MAME Youth Series O.S.O. 1991; All-State Band 1991; Honor Roll student.

References are available on request.

Masoud Ysmiri
211 South Grevillea Avenue, Apt. 26B
Inglewood, California 90301
(213) 555-9562

Objective

Career in electronics design and manufacturing.

Education

Morningside High School, Class of 1992
Cumulative Grade Point Average: 3.9

Pertinent Courses:
* Electronics
* Computer Applications
* Algebra I and II
* Trigonometry
* Pre-calculus
* Science

Experience

Assistant to Electronics Teacher, Morningside HS
Completed all available course work in electronics.
Functioned as lab instructor during beginning
electronics courses, 1990-92.

Achievements

Developed radar device for activating electronic
control panel.

Coordinated project for lighting student theatre.
Built and operated control board for sound and light
productions.

Built and customized computer hard disk drive for
personal computer.

Experienced in repair of stereos, video cassette
recorders, and CD players.

References

Available on request.

Lynn Simmons
2620 House Avenue
Cheyenne, Wyoming 82001
Telephone: 555-2883

Job Sought: Summer firefighting crew.

Education: Central Senior High School
              5500 Education Drive, Cheyenne, Wyoming
              Graduation date June 1993

Training: Hold valid CPR/Lifesaving certificate.

              Trained in firefighting and prevention by local
                 rural fire department.

Experience: U.S. Forest Service, Summer 1990.
                 Spent two weeks with fire crew in Yellowstone
                 National Park on fire damage control. Dug
                 fire trenches, cleared brush, and opened clogged
                 stream beds.

              U.S. Forest Service, Summer 1989.
                 Worked as camp cook's assistant on fire crew on site
                 in Yellowstone National Park. Maintained food
                 provisions for firefighters, assisted with first aid
                 treatment of minor burns, served meals, worked at
                 camp canteen.

References are available at your request.

John Umiak
P.O. Box 1648
Palmer, Alaska 99645
Message phone: 907-555-8406

Objective   Career in fisheries and wildlife.

Education   Susitna Valley Junior-Senior High School
Graduation date: May 1992. GPA 3.6.

My courses have been primarily in biological sciences,
with an emphasis in special projects on salmonid
fishes.

Matanuska-Susitna College

Enrolled in summer 1992 program, taking courses in
general biology and marine biology.

Experience   <u>Matanuska Fisheries</u>, 1990-1992

Worked on fishing boat crew, fishing for salmon,
halibut, crab. Maintained fishing equipment, checked
fishing nets daily for damage and repaired.

<u>Independent Project</u>, 1991-1992.
Coordinated research project on salmon runs on local
stream. Working with my high school biology teacher, I
designed research procedures, collected data, and
discovered a 20% decrease in salmon populations
between 1991 and 1992 spring Chinook runs.

References   Available on request.

Amanda Martin
107226 North 27th
Phoenix, Arizona 85028
(602) 555-3874

Objective   A career in the computer industry.

Education   Shadow Mountain High School, 1988-1992
             Cumulative GPA: 3.75

             Courses emphasized:
             • computer science
             • computer applications
             • computer programming (BASIC, PASCAL)
             • algebra 1 & 2
             • geometry
             • trigonometry
             • pre calculus

Achievements
             • Worked on five-member team to develop new computer
               software for grading multiple-choice tests,
               recording grades, and providing bell curves and
               other averages that could be used for assigning
               letter grades.

             • Customized programming software for use by students
               with sight impairments.

             • Won annual district prize for best computer
               programming solution.

References are available upon request.

Paul Garcia
3836 Sweetwater Avenue
Scottsdale, Arizona 85254
(602) 555-2834

<u>Objective</u>: Summer internship with law office.

<u>Education</u>:

Chaparral High School, class of 1992
Academic standing: 20th in class of 420
Cumulative grade point average: 4.0

Courses taken:
- Business Law
- Business Practices,
- Computer Applications (word processing, spreadsheets, databases, communications)
- Journalism
- Career Options: Law

<u>Achievements</u>:

- BPOE Elks Scholarship
- Zimmerman Scholarship
- Student of the Month, Scottsdale Elks Club
- President, National Honor Society
- Student Senator, Sophomore and Junior years
- Chaparral High Scholarship & Leadership Award
- Dean's Honor Roll
- Member: Chaparral Thespians, Scottsdale First Methodist Church Youth Choir, Chaps (High School Jazz Ensemble)

<u>References</u>: Available on request

Jerome Washington
3705 H Street
Little Rock, Arkansas 72209
501-555-3785

Objective

A career in computer programming and development.

Education

McClellan High School. Graduation Date: May 1992.
Cumulative grade point average: 3.98.

Relevant Courses

*Computer Programming
(BASIC, PASCAL, DOS)
Computer Applications
(Microsoft Word, Lotus 123, dBase, Symphony, Microsoft Works)
Electronics (including microchip technology)
Four years of math*

Honors

*McClellan Senior Scholarship
Little Rock Masonic Scholarship
Most Innovative Computer Solution Award, cBasic Magazine
Elected Treasurer, Computer J's Club*

Work History

Waiter, Genrette's Ice Cream Parlour, 1990-92

Station Attendant, Scott's Chevron, 1989-1990

References are available upon request.

SHAWANA HARRIS
1100 Royal Scots Way, Apt. 245
Bakersfield, California 93306
Telephone: (805) 555-3746
Messages: (805) 555-8892

OBJECTIVE   Customer service job with computer company.

EDUCATION   Foothill High School, 501 Park Drive, Bakersfield
               Expected graduation date: June 1993
               Current GPA: 3.2

               Special courses: computer applications (Microsoft
               Works, WordPerfect, Corel Draw), business practices,
               accounting I.

               Special activities: Served as clerical assistant for
               English teachers. Worked as a clerk in the student
               store. Planned and carried out activities as part of
               the Homecoming and Senior Prom committees. Played
               varsity basketball (top scorer last season). Made
               the honor roll 4 out of 6 semesters.

EXPERIENCE   *Student Assistant,* FHS Computer Lab, 1991-92.
               Worked with computer teacher. Installed and
               initialized software on lab computers. Maintained
               student use records for lab. Assisted students with
               questions about computer software. Supervised check-
               out of lab manuals and materials.

               Waitress, Michael's Landing Restaurant, 1990-92.

REFERENCES   Available on request.

SHARONE DAVIS
22200 Division Street, Apt. 315
Los Angeles, California 93535
(805) 555-3736

OBJECTIVE   Entry level position with production department of newspaper or other printing firm.

EDUCATION   Antelope Valley High School, class of 1992
Cumulative grade point average: 3.48

Pertinent courses: photography, darkroom techniques, graphic design, intro to art, mechanical drawing.

EXPERIENCE

Darkroom Technician, Antelope High School Viewpoint (student newspaper), 1991-92.
Duties: developed, proofed, and printed black-and-white film; prepared PMTs of line art in specified enlargements and reductions; made halftoned prints for direct paste-up; made negatives to size for stripping into plate-ready film.

Paste-up Artist, Antelope High School Viewpoint, 1990-91.
Duties: pasted typeset copy into position on paste-up boards; used light table to crop halftone photographs; used border tape for graphic boxes and framing of photographs; used Compugraphic headliner to create headlines for news articles. Completed first two phases of training on computerized layout with Macintosh computer and Quark XPress layout software.

REFERENCES are available on request.

Michael Han
435 S. Monaco Parkway
Denver, Colorado 80204
(303) 555-4481

Education

West High School, 951 Elati Street, Denver. 1988-92.   Diploma. G.P.A.: 3.86.

Aachen Gymnasium, Bonn, West Germany, 1990-91 (Exchange Student).

Blevins Junior High School, 2101 S. Taft Road, Fort Collins. 1986-88. G.P.A.: 4.0.

Skills & Achievements

* Trained in basic bookkeeping, invoicing, inventory, and payroll procedures.
* Speak fluent Chinese and German; working knowledge of French.
* Experienced with various computer software and hardware, including MS Dos, Macintosh, and CP/M operating platforms; WordPerfect, Microsoft Word, and MacWrite word processing; Lotus 1-2-3 and Works spreadsheet; and dBase and Filemaker Pro database software, among others.
* Experienced with providing customer service in a small retail sales outlet for computer equipment.
* Excellent writing and communications skills.
* Effective leadership skills: served as president of senior class, vice president of junior class, student senator during freshman and sophomore years.
* Selected by American Field Service (AFS) as exchange student to Aachen, West Germany.

Employment History

Summer Sales Intern, Computer Express, Denver. Winter 1991-92.
Duties: Provide information and assistance to clients in small computer hardware and software dealership that handled both IBMs and compatibles and Macintosh computers. Self-trained in a wide range of software in order to better match appropriate software and hardware systems to clients' needs.

References available on request.

Mark Bettorini
2100 West Oxford Avenue
Englewood, Colorado 80110
(303) 555-3422

Objective   Career in forestry/wood products industry that will utilize my science background, timber experience, and leadership skills.

Experience

Fire Watch/Tree Planter, U.S. Forest Service, Denver. Summer 1992

Crew Leader, Colorado Highway Department, Grounds Crew. Summer 1991

Education

Sheridan High School, Englewood
Class of 1993
Major: Science

Leadership

Student Body Vice-President, Sheridan High School, 1991-92
President, Sheridan Hikers Club, 1990-91
President, American Junior Red Cross, 1992
Vice President, Science Club, 1990-92
Captain, Sheridan High School Archery Team, 1991-92
Founding Member, Sheridan High Key Club (volunteer service club), 1990

Honors

Junior Science Student of the Year, 1992
Rotary Club International Exchange Student to New Zealand, Spring 1991
Key Club Volunteer of the Month, December 1991

References are available on request.

JUDY REIMER
128 Orange Street
New Haven, CT 06510
(203) 555-3754

OBJECTIVE

To secure a position as a paralegal where my education and writing and research skills can be utilized to enhance the effectiveness of a small- to medium-sized law firm.

EDUCATION

Hillhouse High School, 480 Sherman Parkway, New Haven; diploma awarded May 1992.

Concentration: business law, accounting I and II, computer applications (word processing, spreadsheet, database, and communications software for MS DOS operating platforms), business operations (clerical systems). Cumulative GPA: 3.75.

EXPERIENCE

Office Assistant. Switter, Harvey, Jenkins, & Hewitt, Attorneys at Law, 1990-present.

Duties: Assisted attorneys and legal secretaries. Typed and proofed legal forms. Answered telephone calls on ten-line switchboard. Organized office law library and reshelved books.

Student Assistant. Hillhouse High School, Junior Office, 1989-90.

Duties: Assisted staff secretaries with typing, filing, answering telephones, and duplication. Distributed mail to teachers and administrators. Distributed completed work orders to teachers. Operated stencil machine, ditto machine, photocopier, fax machine, and six-line switchboard.

ACTIVITIES & ACHIEVEMENTS

Secretary, National Honor Society, 1991-92
Copy Editor, Sheridan High School Annual, 1990-91
Senior Editor, Sheridan High School Annual, 1991-92
Team Captain, Sheridan High School Girls Softball Team, 1991-92
Member, Future Business Leaders of America, 1988-1990
Member, Thespians (participated in three play productions), 1988-91

REFERENCES

Available on request

STUART J. ECK
126 S. Granby
Hartford, Connecticut 06112
203-555-6623

EDUCATION:
- Bulkeley High School, 300 Wethersfield Avenue, Hartford
  Class of 1993.

- Hold 4.0 grade point average in all math, business, writing, and English courses.

- Recipient of Who's Who Among American High School Students

LEADERSHIP:
- Presided over school Business Club. Planned programs, managed budget, set meeting agendas, and organized meetings and club activities. 1991-92.

- Elected Secretary of the Student Senate. Responsible for maintaining Roberts Rules of Order. 1991-92.

- Managed budget, personnel time sheets, and all-school database for student publication. Used Microsoft Works software on Macintosh computers. 1991-92.

- Received full scholarship to attend Boys State at State Capitol. Summer 1990.

- Supervised volunteer labor while working at Hartford's Capitol grounds. Spring 1990.

EXPERIENCE:
- *Business Manager*, The Hart (student annual), 1991-92.

- *Groundskeeper*, Bulkeley High School, 1989-91.

- *Corpsmember*, U.S. Federal Government, Youth Conservation Corps, 1989-90.

REFERENCES AVAILABLE UPON REQUEST

Craig Kohanek
1851 S. Edwards Road, No. 59
Wilmington, Delaware 19809
302-555-7229; Message: 302-555-1762

OBJECTIVE

To obtain a position in sales in an organization oriented toward customer service.

EDUCATION

Mount Pleasant High School, Washington Boulevard, Wilmington. Class of 1993.

Course of study: Business I and II (organizational structures, economics of business, business ethics, business law, personnel management, business regulations), Computer Systems (software applications in word processing, database management, accounting, and communications), Office Management (clerical operations, bookkeeping, basic accounting).

EXPERIENCE

Library Assistant, Mt. Pleasant High School Senior Library, January 1990 - present.
Organize and record use of magazines in periodicals section. Instruct students on library research techniques and microfilm usage. Answer questions. Maintain copy machine. Reshelve books.

Cashier, Hartford Country Club Golf Shop. June - September 1991. Sold rounds of golf, clubs, shoes, and miscellaneous equipment. Monitored driving range. Supervised and participated in cleaning and maintenance of clubhouse.

Retail Sales Clerk, Sam's Shoe Shop, Hartford. June - September 1989 and 1990. Trained in sales and customer service. Greeted customers, took measurements, assisted with style and color selection, ran cash register. Received and accounted for delivered merchandise on corresponding purchase orders and invoices. Designed and set up seasonal displays.

LEADERSHIP EXPERIENCE

Student Tutor, Mt. Pleasant High School, English classes, 1989 - 1992
Student Representative, Mt. Pleasant High School, Student Senate, 1990 - 1992
Competitor, Mt. Pleasant High School, Forensics Squad, 1989 - 1992
Representative, Mt. Pleasant High School Model United Nations, 1992

EXTRACURRICULAR ACTIVITIES

Varsity Basketball, Mt. Pleasant High School, 1990 - 1992
Concert Choir, First United Church, 1987 - present
Varsity Cross Country, 1990 - 1992
Golf enthusiast

REFERENCES AVAILABLE UPON REQUEST

Mary Jo Baptiste
2240 N.W. Nebraska Avenue
Washington, D.C. 20016
202-555-7465

OBJECTIVE

To obtain a training position as a preschool guide in a Montessori preschool.

EDUCATIONAL BACKGROUND

Coolidge High School, Washington, D.C.
Graduation date: June 1993

Relevant Courses: Human Development, Childhood Education, Psychology, Sociology, Social Science, Speech and Communications.

Honors: Who's Who Among American High School Students, Future Teachers of America, Volunteer Student Activist of the Year (all-school nomination), District of Columbia Youth of the Month (President's Council on Youth), Quill and Scroll (journalism honorary).

EXPERIENCE

Parks & Recreation Day Camp Leader, Washington, D.C., Summer 1990 and 1991.
Planned programs for children 4-8 years old. Built rapport and communications with parents. Provided supervision of children on play structures during breaks. Taught teamwork skills through problem solving in groups of six children. Taught crafts, songs, and dances. Taught storytelling to children aged 10-14.

Outdoor School Counselor and Instructor, D.C. School District, 1989 - 1992.
Counseled, supervised, and instructed sixth-grade students from various Washington elementary schools during one-week program each Spring. Assumed responsibility for twelve girls. Served as live-in counselor three years, one year as instructor emphasizing environmental education and human influences.

Other part-time employment: Waitress, housekeeper, clerical assistant.

SPECIAL SKILLS AND INTERESTS

Reporter for two years on the high school newspaper staff. Published an article in the *City Paper,* Washington, D.C., February 1992. Knowledgeable of Native American culture, including traditional songs, dances, and crafts.

References are available upon request.

Jennette Bouchardon
21 Lawrence Street N.W.
Washington, D.C. 20017
(202) 555-2951

Objective

To obtain a position in an international business where my bilingual skills and experience in sales and customer service will be used to advantage.

Experience

Holiday Inn Corporation, Washington, 1991 and 1992 (summers)
Assistant Night Manager
• Assisted with translation for French-speaking guests
• Coordinated night-shift activities
• Managed front-desk operations
• Operated telephone switchboard and reservations desk
• Conducted night audits of front desk register

La Maison Bleu, Washington, 1991-92 (part-time)
Hostess
• Assisted with translation for French-speaking guests
• Supervised cash register
• Supervised table seating
• Supervised bussing staff

Nordstrom's Department Store, 1990-1991 (weekends)
Salesperson
• Sold women's sportswear, cosmetics, and jewelry
• Maintained accurate balance sheets, accounting for all sales
• Recipient of August 1991 Sales Award (based on per-work-hour sales)

Education

Washington International School, 3100 MaComb Street, N.W., Washington
• Honors student with cumulative grade point average of 5.8 (6.0 scale).
• Anticipated date of graduation: May 1993.

Special Skills

• Fluent French speaker (child of French parents; mother member of Corps Diplomatique)
• Excellent interpersonal communications skills
• General knowledge of import-export restrictions between U.S. and E.E.C.

References

Available on request.

Sharon Flaherty
1250 Harvard Street N.W.
Washington, D.C. 20009
(202) 555-4119

Objective   To obtain a position as an assistant librarian where I can utilize my interpersonal and organizational skills.

Education

St. Anselms Abbey School, Washington, D.C., Class of 1992

Relevant Courses Taken:
* Business
* Office Systems
* Computers in Business
* Research Strategies
* English / Writing (four years)

Experience

Student Librarian, St. Anselms Academy, October 1990 - May 1992.

Responsibilities:

* Checked books out to students and teachers

* Maintained records of books on loan

* Checked returned books against borrowing records

* Advised students on research techniques using the library

* Assisted students in the use of the card catalog

* Assisted users with computer database

* Answered questions about reference materials

* Maintained accurate shelving of books and periodicals

Special Skills and Achievements

* Experienced with on-line database references for library use (Reader's Guide to Periodical Literature, Business Periodicals Index, Science Periodicals Index, among others).

* Selected High School Student of the Month (March 1991) for ongoing volunteer activities with Stone Soup, an urban hunger project.

* Experienced with use of computers for word processing, page layout, and data base management (WriteNow, Word Perfect, Print Shop, and Microsoft Works).

* Listed on Honor Roll each year; member of National Honor Society.

References are available at your request.

Claire Renard

618 N.W. Eighth Street, No. 215
Boca Raton, Florida 33486
Telephone: 555-1400

Objective

To obtain a position that will lead to a career in banking, where my skills in finance, accounting, and organization can be effectively utilized.

Education

Boca Raton High School, 1501 N.W. Fifteenth Street. Class of 1992.

Pertinent Courses: Business I and II, Economics, Accounting I and II, Business Writing, Office Management Systems, Typing I and II

Achievements

Elected Student Body Treasurer. Chaired Finance Committee. Maintained student account books. Recorded income from student fund drives and disbursements for student charities and activities. 1991-92

Served on the Finance Committee for the Student Government. 1990-91

Coordinated Student Fund Drive which raised 20 percent more than the previous year's drive to benefit children's programs in Palm Beach County. Served as liaison with local community service center for direction of funds disbursement. 1990-91

Acted as Committee Representative to Student Body Executive Board. Attended meetings and presented financial reports to student body officers and advisors. 1990-91

Elected President of Business Club. Coordinated monthly meetings. Supervised planning for Business Career Day. 1991-92

Served as Treasurer of the Debate Club. Maintained records of dues and expenses for field trips and school visitations. 1989-90

Working knowledge of French. Completed four years of high school French and spent one month living in Quebec as part of an intensive language program.

Other Activities

Member of National Honor Society, Girl's Cross Country Track Team, Social Committee, Club Français, Homecoming Committee, Young Life

References

Available on request

Gretchen Morrison
2606 Chelsea Street
Tampa, Florida 33603
813-555-8220

<u>Objective</u>	Entry-level position that will lead to a career in social service.
<u>Education</u>	Temple Heights Christian School, Tampa Graduation date: May 1993 <u>Relevant course work</u>: human development, education, social science, public government, civics, speech communication
<u>Experience</u>	<u>Volunteer Coordinator</u>, Project Second Wind, Tampa Central District, 1992 <u>Duties</u>: Coordinated volunteers from five Tampa high schools. Planned strategies for publicity, volunteer solicitation, site coordination, and area canvassing. Plotted maps for canvassing communities. Worked with National Guard dispatch office to coordinate drivers for collecting food donations through canvassing. On day of drive, supervised canvassing efforts for the five areas. Coordinated delivery to central warehouse. <u>Volunteer</u>, Meals on Wheels, Tampa, 1989-91 <u>Duties</u>: Prepare individual meal servings for weekly delivery to invalids in Tampa area. Deliver meals and visit with invalids. <u>Counselor</u>, Summer Camp, Tampa Heights Christian School, 1990-92 <u>Duties</u>: Assumed responsibility for twelve girls aged 8 to 12. Prepared and presented lessons in Bible study and environmentalism. Taught canoeing. Provided guitar accompaniment for camp sing-alongs.
<u>Activities</u>	Active member of Say No club, which sponsored drug awareness programs at local elementary schools. Worked with student committees to plan social events. Helped with publicity for student elections. Played on softball team sponsored by local business.
<u>References</u>	Available on request.

Jameson W. Brussard, Jr.
212 N. Jefferson Street
Albany, Georgia 31701
(912) 555-2239

Objective   A position in customer service leading to a career in business management.

Sales Experience

Served as salesperson in sporting goods store. Over six-month period, made consistent increases in sales, which led to my being selected as salesperson of the quarter, spring 1992.

Sold compact discs and cassettes for a music store. Maintained position among top ten salespeople. Became very knowledgeable about both classical and contemporary music.

Leadership

Elected Senior Class Vice President, 1991-92. Responsible for overseeing committees, served as senior class representative to Student Senate. Assumed responsibilities of class President in her absence.

Revived Business Club; served as President, 1991-92. Set meeting agendas, presided over meetings, instituted fund drive to sponsor professional visitations and field trips, organized trips to local business organizations.

Management

Managed Student Store, Monroe High School, 1991-92. Supervised student clerks, scheduled work shifts, ordered supplies, received shipments and checked them against purchase orders, served customers.

Served as Weekend Night Manager at a 125-room motel. Greeted guests, managed registration desk, supervised night staff, and served as security representative on alternating weekends.

Work History

Weekend Night Manager, Motel Orleans, Albany, Georgia, July 1992 - present
Salesperson, Jefferson's Sporting Goods, Albany, Georgia, May 1991 - June 1992
Salesperson, Musicland, Albany, Georgia. June 1989 - May 1991

Education

Monroe High School, Albany, Georgia
Graduation class of 1993

Activities & Memberships: Business Club, Forensics Club, National Honor Society, Pep Club, Publicity Committee, Photography Club, JV and Varsity Wrestling

References

Available on request

SAMUEL JUN-LAN CHEN
2110 Cottage Grove Avenue
Chicago Heights, Illinois 60411
Telephone: 708-555-2645

OBJECTIVE	To obtain a laboratory research assistant position in a scientific lab.
EDUCATION	Bloom High School, 101 West Tenth Street, Chicago Heights, Illinois Graduated with highest honors, 1992. Cumulative GPA: 3.96.

RELEVANT COURSES TAKEN:
- Biology (two years)
- General Chemistry (one year)
- Organic Chemistry (one year)
- Physics (one year)
- Botany (one semester)
- Math (algebra, trigonometry, calculus)

EXPERIENCE   Laboratory Assistant, Bloom High School, Chemistry Section, 1991-92
- Assisted teacher with laboratory preparation and set-up
- Answered student questions about laboratory experiments
- Graded lab worksheets and recorded grades for chemistry teacher
- Maintained chemical stock room and kept track of supplies

Laboratory Assistant, Bloom High School, Biology Section, 1990-91
- Assisted with laboratory preparation and clean up
- Worked with students on dissection projects (frog, fetal pig heart)
- Graded student lab worksheets
- Installed and tested new computer software for simulated dissection
- Directed students in use of computer software

ACTIVITIES
- Member of Future Scientists of America
- Secretary, Bloom High Science Club
- Coordinated visitation day for seven scientists from Chicago-area research institutions and manufacturing companies
- Served as general science assistant for science teachers

REFERENCES
- Available on request.

§   S T E W A R T   S U L L I V A N   §

O B J E C T I V E   To secure a position on the production staff of a printing company where I may utilize my skills with graphic design, typesetting, and layout.

E X P E R I E N C E   Graphic Artist, Student Yearbook Staff, 1990-92

§   Assumed responsibility for overall design concepts in 212-page hardbound yearbook.

§   Provided design assistance to editorial staff. Developed graphic elements for pages needing art work.

§   Designed page layouts and prepared camera-ready mechanicals.

§   First year, used all traditional layout and paste-up methods. Second year, incorporated computer page-layout technology with desktop publishing software.

§   Prepared photographs for publication (cropped, sized)

§   Supervised staff of production assistants.

Production Assistant, Borah Gazette, 1989-91

§   Prepared paste-up boards for student newspaper.

§   Used light table to crop screened photographs.

§   Designed graphics for accenting advertisement section.

Typesetter, Borah Gazette, 1989-90

§   Input copy and headlines on Compugraphic 2420, using appropriate codes for setting line length, type fonts and styles, and type sizes.

E D U C A T I O N   Borah Senior High School, Boise, Idaho
Class of 1993. Grade point average in art: 4.0.

Areas of study: Journalism, Photojournalism, Graphic Design, Art (painting, drawing, watercolor, ceramics)

R E F E R E N C E S   Available on request.

1220 North Cole Road   §   Boise, Idaho 83709   §   555-2477

Joanna C. Harper
1150 S. 16th St.
Decatur, Illinois 62521
708-555-2366

Job Sought   Word processing operator, full-time summer employment.

Education and Training

MacArthur High School, Decatur, Illinois   Graduation: June 1993

My major area of emphasis has been business, with course work in office procedures, business machines, business communications, keyboarding (beginning and advanced), computer applications, and accounting I.

Specific training includes computer graphics, word processing, data processing, and electronic spreadsheet. I have also received some basic instruction in desktop publishing. My word processing speed is 65 words per minute, and I operate a 10-key adding machine at approximately 35 numbers per minute.

Work Experience

James Brophy, D.D.S.   Summer 1991
1267 S. 15th St., Decatur, Illinois 62521; 708-424-0112
Supervisor: Mrs. Dionne Avery

Job duties: assisted with word processing, filing, typing, answering telephones, scheduling appointments, and managing the reception desk.

Mrs. Arva Ellison   1986-1991
7878 S. Cantrell St., Decatur, Illinois 65251; 708-424-3349
Job duties: provided part-time and summer full-time child care for three children.

Ellison Farms   Summer 1988, 1989
7878 S. Cantrell St., Decatur, Illinois 65251; 708-424-3356
Job duties: operated seeder, assisted with harvest of a variety of crops, assisted with irrigation systems, and provided general labor.

Activities

Varsity Rally Squad: Basketball
Played flute in Concert Band
Recreational Cross Country Ski Club
Drama Club

References   Available on request

Parker Adams
226 N. Fifth Street, Apt. 42
Fairbury, Illinois 61739
Telephone: 815-555-1154

Position Desired:

Lab assistant, seed cleaning, full-time summer employment. My long-term career goal is to be a bio-medical engineer.

Education and Training:

Prairie Central High School, Fairbury, Illinois. Graduation anticipated June 1993.

My major area of emphasis has been science. During the past three years I have completed all of the science courses offered at PCHS, including: biology, chemistry, anatomy and physiology, physics, earth science, field biology, horticulture, and advanced chemistry. I have participated in extra-credit research projects in most of these courses.
Science grade point average: 3.68.

Experience:

Organization: As a lab assistant in the science program, I have organized labs, maintained inventory of supplies, entered data into the computer, and assisted students with class assignments.

Equipment: I have operated microscopes, digital meters, and oscilloscopes. I also drive a tractor when working on my grandfather's seed farm.

Efficiency: During my junior year, I worked as a laborer on the family farm approximately 20 hours per week. I was concurrently working on a special science honors project which required several hours each week of after-school study. I was able to manage my time efficiently and maintain a 3.9 grade point average for the year.

Honors:

First Place Project Award, Science VII, Regional Skills Conference, 1992
Honorable Mention, Science VI, Regional Skills Conference, 1991

References are available upon request.

Laura Chen
5527 N. W. Oak Creek Road
Ashland, Oregon 97520
(503) 555-9982

Job Sought: Entry level position in the field of environmental economics.

Education & Training:

Mt. Ashland Senior High School   Graduation Class of 1992
Ashland, Oregon 97520   Cumulative GPA: 3.95

Science & Math Courses: Business & Economics Courses
- Earth Science   • Business Communications
- Horticulture   • Economics & Government
- Biology   • Capstone Economics
- Algebra 1 & 2   • Computer Applications
- Probability & Statistics   • Computer Keyboarding

Work Experience:

Prudential Bache Securities   Internship, Summer 1991
One Union Square, Suite 2400, Seattle, Washington 98101
Supervisor: Kathryn Mix, (205) 623-9111

Duties: Posted account records in ledger and conducted research on major
corporations. Major area of interest was product liability suits against corporations
filing Chapter 11 to escape same suit.

Brown's Steak House   October 1990 to present
17 First Street, Ashland, Oregon 97520
Supervisor: Joseph Brown, (503) 486-2219

Duties: Hostess in charge of seating clients at the restaurant during peak evening
hours. Manage cashier's station. Work part-time while going to school.

Oregon River Experience   Summer 1988 to present
34497 Tall Pines Drive, Grants Pass, Oregon 97526
Supervisor: John Hendersen (503) 486-2294

Duties: From May to October (with the exception of 1991) I have worked either as
a lead guide or a support guide. As lead guide, I lead raft trips down the Rogue
River, organize equipment and travel logistics, plan and cook menus, and am
responsible for knowledge of the river and surrounding area as well as for the safety
and equipment of a group of 25 to 30 people for two to five days. As a support
guide, I assist the lead guide in carrying out these responsibilities and row the
supply boat.

Awards

Top three percent of graduating class; National Honor Society; Economics
Honorary; Prudential Bache Internship (a merit award based on Northwest regional
competition)

References are available upon request.

Patrick O'Callahan
1806 N. Washington Avenue, Apartment 362
Evansville, Indiana 47711-2298
Telephone: (812) 555-2295
Message: (812) 555-2983

Objective   Career in business administration and management.

Education   North High School, Evansville, Indiana.   Graduating Class of 1993

My course program has centered on a business and management curriculum. Specific courses include: business law, business management, economics, accounting 1-2-3, leadership, public speaking, psychology, sociology, personal relationships, and Japanese. My grade point average in these areas is 3.83.

**Communication
Skills:**   Completed three years of language arts courses, including advanced composition and business communications.

Arranged and directed student discussion panel on global issues.

Interacted successfully with the public in positions as a sales representative and a part-time waiter.

Served as campaign coordinator for successful student body presidential candidate.

Participated in debate team and forensics squad. Won two regional first-place awards in debate and three second-place awards in persuasive speaking.

**Leadership and Organizational
Skills**

Served two terms as student president for Junior Achievement. During that time membership increased 23 percent, and our organization was named best in the state. Established subcommittees to target membership drives and continue organizational development.

Served as treasurer of Future Business Leaders of America, Evansville Regional Chapter. Coordinated joint activities among Bosse, Central, Harrison, North, and Reitz High Schools. Coordinated business career fair at city convention center. Worked with committee chairs to coordinate school visitations to promote business to junior high schools.

Experience   Sales Representative   Summers 1990-92
Prange's Department Store, Boy's Sportswear
Supervisor: Joey Ableman

Waiter   May 1989-June 1990
The Fish House
Supervisor: Annette Townsend

References   Available on request.

Dylan James McDonald
1415 Wenig Road N.E.
Cedar Rapids, Iowa 52402
(319) 555-2284

**Occupational
Objective**
To obtain an entry-level position with a computer software manufacturer where my skills in computer programming and applications might lead to advancement in program design.

**Educational
Background**
Metro High School, Cedar Rapids, Iowa   Current Status: Senior
Computer Science GPA: 4.0   Cumulative GPA: 3.66

**Computer
Expertise**
Completed three semesters of computer programming.
Developed programming projects individually and in teams.
Proficient in BASIC, PASCAL, and Hypercard programming languages.
Initiated self-study FORTRAN program project.
Experienced with word processing, spreadsheet, and database programs.
Working knowledge of desktop publishing and graphic design software.
Highly experienced with MS DOS operating platforms.
Basic knowledge of and some experience with UNIX-based systems.
Worked on NEXT computer system for three months on special project.

**Work
History**
Administrative Assistant, Health Care Nursing Center, Cedar Rapids
                                              June 1990 to present
Served as swing shift assistant manager for 60-bed facility. Supervised maintenance personnel. Also responsible for some support services, including patient form processing, database management, record keeping, and filing.

Young Men's Christian Association, Cedar Rapids
                                          September 1989 to June 1990
Supervised various evening recreational activities in facility that included swimming pool, shuffleboard, ping pong, bowling lanes, and a gymnasium. Responsible for equipment check-out and locker room inspections.

**Extracurricular
Activities**
Vice President, Keyboard Club (member since 1989; V.P. 1991-92)
Peer tutor, mathematics
Young Life
Student Empowerment Training Project (STEP) Leadership Training

**Honors &
Awards**
YMCA Youth of the Month, June 1990
Computer Programming Award, Science VII Regional Competition
National Honor Society Scholar of the Month

References
Available on request

Asher Toppman
10220 Goodwood Boulevard
Baton Rouge, Louisiana 70802
(504) 555-8820

Career Objective   To become an efficient and effective legal assistant while beginning preparations for entering college pre-law program.

Education   Broadmoor High School, Baton Rouge, Louisiana
Current status: Senior
Current GPA: 3.98

Leadership   President, Associated Student Body of Broadmoor High School, 1992-93

Junior Class President, BHS, 1991-92

Sophomore Class Vice President, BHS, 1990-91

Freshman Student Senate Representative, Social Studies, 1989-90

President, Forensics Team, 1990-91

News Director, Radio Club, 1991-92

Communication   Completed six semesters in writing and communication courses.

Presented numerous speeches in forensics competition.

Presented campaign speeches for elected offices.

Won Young Democrats of America essay contest, 1992.

Completed exploratory honors project in radio broadcasting.

Served as news director for weekly 15-minute radio show on WBTR, produced by Radio Club.

Organization   Directed planning and execution of several student events while serving as student body president and junior class president.

Served on student senate ethics committee, which sponsored Honor Day and a "drug-free zone" day.

Developed editorial procedures for planning weekly news broadcasts with other radio club officers.

Honors   Kiwanis Club Scholarship Designee, 1992
Honors Program, Best Project Award, 1991
Merit Scholar, Broadmoor PTA, 1990, 1991, 1992

References are available on request.

Tristan Swanson
19 Malta Street
Augusta, Maine 04330
(207) 555-0119

Objective

A career in media communications where my writing and
editorial skills will be utilized to advantage.

Education

Cony High School, Augusta, Maine   Anticipated Graduation: May 1993
Major Area of Study: Journalism and Communications   Cumulative GPA: 3.56

Writing Experience

• Activities and Entertainment Editor, *Cony Crier*, student newspaper, junior year.

• Wrote monthly column for local city newspaper, *Kennebec Journal*, high school page.

• Worked as reporter for the *Cony Crier* since freshman year.

• Completed two years of specialized course work in journalism and media communications.

• Wrote script for documentary film on ocean pollution on the Eastern Seaboard.

• Won publication of two poems in National Young Poets '91 competition, Boston, Mass.

Leadership Experience

• Served as social committee chairman for student body of Cony High School. Planned various social events such as dances, barbecues, pep rallies, and a speaker's forum.

• Active in Letterman's Club, a service club of varsity sports players. Organized food drives and raffle to benefit Hunger Project.

• Captain, Varsity Basketball Team. Responsible for encouraging players in pre-game and post-practice activities.

Work History

• Bath Cove Fleet, Bath, Maine. Worked on a fishing boat as cook's helper and crew member. Summers, 1990-1992.

• Burger King, Augusta, Maine. Worked as kitchen staff and line cook part-time while attending school. September 1991-May 1992.

References are available on request.

Allison Barnes
2880 West Braddock Road
Alexandria, Virginia 22302
Telephone: 703-555-1283

Career Objective	To obtain a position with a small theatre company where my background in theatre will allow me to make contributions in a variety of areas.
Experience	Directed production of Arthur Miller's "Death of a Salesman." Took play to state drama competition and received honorable mention.
	Played Lisl in Community Theatre production of "The Sound of Music." Won the part from among 84 auditioners.
	Designed sets and costumes, and worked on costume and set building crews, for a production of Shakespeare's "Twelfth Night."
	Sang the lead in "Oklahoma."
	Played a walk-on part in "Our Town." Served back stage as key grip.
	Assisted with design and production of lighting for "Faculty Follies," an entirely student-directed production starring teachers, counselors, and administrators from throughout the high school.
	Operated video cameras during dress rehearsals for "Our Town" and "Twelfth Night."
	Wrote reviews of local theatre (non-school) productions for student newspaper. One review was published in the weekend edition of the *Alexandria Gazette*.
Education	Williams Senior High School, Alexandria, Virginia, Class of 1993
	Courses included: Drama, Advanced Drama, Play Writing, Special Projects: Theatre, Shakespeare, Creative Writing, Advanced Composition, and Journalism.
Work History	Waitress, New Morning Cafe, Alexandria January 1990 - present
References	Available upon request

SUZANNE BARSTOW
2248 W. Billtown Road, Apt. 16
Louisville, Kentucky 40215
502/555-7751

JOB OBJECTIVE

A part-time position as nurse's assistant in a hospital or health care facility. My long-term career goal is to become a pediatrician.

EXPERIENCE

Candy Striper, Louisville General Hospital   Volunteer 1989 - present

Duties: Assist nurses with distribution of medication, visit with patients, deliver reading materials and other items at patient's requests, provide general assistance to nursing staff.

EDUCATION

Iriquois High School, Taylor Boulevard, Louisville   Class of 1993
Major course of study: Health and Physical Education   Current GPA: 3.89

Courses Completed: anatomy and physiology, basic health, personal health: wellness, CPR-first aid, childhood development, advanced foods and nutrition.

COMMUNICATION SKILLS

Completed three semesters of courses that specialized in written and oral business communication.

Served as school spirit committee chair. Built sense of school spirit by establishing pep section for all athletic events. Coordinated with school band and rally squads to encourage participation.

Participated for two semesters in forensics, presenting a variety of speeches on topics ranging from personal health and fitness to the war in the Persian Gulf.

INTERPERSONAL SKILLS

Attentive listener, able to lend a sympathetic, nonjudgmental ear when needed.

Able to gain trust and rapport with various types of individuals.

Concerned and empathetic, willing to help those in need.

HONORS

Member of the National Honor Society

Selected Candy Striper of the Month, Louisville General Hospital

Placed second in state forensics competition, exposition category

REFERENCES AVAILABLE ON REQUEST

Joshua Whitely
228 West Fifth Street
P.O. Box 286
Emporia, Kansas 66801
555-2251

Job Sought   Full-time summer position with manufacturing company or warehouse.

Education   Emporia High School, Emporia, Kansas
Class of 1994

Experience   Jayhawk Auto Parts, Emporia
Clerk, Summers 1990 and 1991

Duties: Serve customers, answer questions about auto parts and other merchandise, maintain order in stockroom, find parts by order number on stock shelves, remove items sold from computer inventory, assist with receiving shipments and entering new stock in computer inventory.

Activities   Varsity and junior varsity sports: football, basketball, and baseball
Freshman football, cross country
Key Club
Spirit Club
EHS Tech

References   Available on request.

McHale Newport
2200 River Road, No. 126
Annapolis, Maryland 21401
301/555-8461

Professional Goal

To obtain an entry-level position in the news department of a daily newspaper where I can utilize my journalistic skills and professionalism.

Education

Broadneck Senior High School
1265 Green Holly Drive, Annapolis, Maryland
Class of 1993

Writing Experience

Student Reporter, The BSHS Times, Broadneck High School, 1989 - present

Wrote articles on student government, administrative decisions, school board meetings, student activities, sports events, and profiles of student leaders and teachers. Entered copy on computer word processing software. Served one semester as interim editor, determined story assignments for student reporters, worked with adviser on writing editorials, and edited news copy submitted by student reporters. Served as staff photographer on several occasions.

Freelance Writer, 1991 to present

Published two articles in the "Teen Beat" section of The Capital (Annapolis daily newspaper). Published one personality profile of the high school principal in *American Teen* magazine. Submitted several query letters and manuscripts to a variety of magazines for publication.

Activities

Junior Press Club of Annapolis (a local high school division of the Maryland Press Club)
The Lancer, Broadneck SHS student annual (helped with photography, layout, editing)
Aperture (Photography Club)

References and portfolio of writing and photography are available on request.

Mary Alice Simpson
1280 Delaware Avenue, Apt. 116
Buffalo, New York 24214
716/555-8482

Objective

I am seeking an internship with a business enterprise where my skills in writing and communications may contribute to the effectiveness of the organization.

Education

Holy Angels Academy, 24 Shoshone Street, Buffalo, New York 14214
Class of 1993
Cumulative Grade Point Average: 3.38

Course of Study

My high school curriculum has focused on gaining a broad background in liberal studies and business in preparation for attending college. In addition to course work in business, management, and accounting, I participated in the college preparatory honors program, which offered intensive courses in U.S. and European History, English Composition, Research Methods, and Social Science.

Achievements & Activities

Selected to serve as senior monitor for academic testing programs

Served on student government committee for finance. Conducted several successful campaigns to raise funds for school programs.

Participated in the a capella choir, madrigals singers, and concert choir.

Assisted with parent night preparations and planning.

Member of the Quill staff, which published a school literary magazine.

Published three poems in Quill.

References are available on request.

Tamara Su Sutterby
2404 Gallant Road
Charlotte, NC   28216
(704) 555-2119

Objective   To obtain a position as a receptionist or clerical specialist.

Education   Central High School, Charlotte, North Carolina
Graduation date: June 1992

Courses taken:
• Keyboarding Skill Building (65 w.p.m.)
• Computer Applications
• Business Machines
• Word Processing, Word Perfect
• Office Systems
• Business Communications

Experience   **Clerical Assistant,** Central High School, Charlotte, Jan.-Mar. 1992
Worked with office staff as part of cooperative work experience program for
class credit. Enhanced office and business skills through on-the-job learning.
Duties included filing, typing, answering telephones, and serving as front
desk receptionist.

Cashier, Wendy's Restaurant, Charlotte, June-Aug. 1991
Worked front line cashier station and drive-through window. Greeted
customers, collected prepared food according to orders, handled money,
balanced cash drawer.

Activities   Ski Club, Young Republicans of North Carolina, Pep Club, Varsity Wrestling
Rally, Drama Club, Girls Choir

References   Available on request.

Robin Weiss
2250 Second Avenue
Akron, Ohio 44313
Telephone: 216-555-9941

Job Sought   Sales clerk with sporting goods or department store.

Education

                    <u>Firestone High School</u>
                    Class of '93.

Experience

                    <u>Sales Clerk</u>, Firestone Student Store, 9/92-present
                    Operated student store sales. Handled cash
                    exchanges and credit account charges. Balanced
                    daily receipts.

                    <u>Referee</u>, Summit County Soccer Clubs, 1989-92
                    Served as referee for elementary and junior high
                    school level soccer games.

Special Skills
                    Trained in CPR and advanced life saving.

                    Knowledgeable about a wide variety of outdoor
                    sports.

Interests &
Activities   Recreational Water Sports Club
                    Outdoor School Counselor
                    Explorers Club
                    Canoe and kayak river trips, water polo, hiking,
                        cycling, archery

References   Available on request

Brenda Pitt-Williams

3488 Chester Avenue
Philadelphia, Pennsylvania 19151
Messages: 215/555-7741

Objective	Nurse's Aide in health care organization.
Education	Friends Central School North 68th and City Avenue Philadelphia, PA 19151 Graduate, 1992
Abilities	Trained in CPR and emergency first aid. Experienced in working with invalids. Completed course work in human anatomy and physiology. Studied nutrition and stress management. Worked with children involved in crisis intervention. Experienced in maintaining antiseptic environment.
Experience	Volunteer, Cheltenham Nursing Home Visited with elderly invalids. Read letters and newspapers to those who needed assistance. Helped maintenance staff with maintaining cleanliness. Assisted nursing staff with rounds and distribution of medication. 1990-present.
	Volunteer, Women's Shelter, operated by the Friends Society. Helped children of women staying at the shelter adjust to changes. Gathered donations of toys and games and played with children of all ages. 1989-1992
	Babysitter, various private individuals. Provided child care for several children, from three months to twelve years of age. Cared for up to seven children at a time. 1986-present.
Activities	Scholarship and Leadership Committee Volunteer Assistance League Friends for Peaceful Conflict Resolution, Junior Chapter Study Session Leader Peer Tutor, English and history

References are available upon request.

Burke Anderson

260 E. North Avenue
Baltimore, Maryland 21202
301/555-4458

Objective   A career in technology design and development that will utilize my skills in
technology innovation and traditional and computer-aided drafting.

Education   Baltimore City College High School, Baltimore, Maryland
Major area of study: science and technology
Major courses G.P.A.: 6.0. (scale of 6) Cumulative G.P.A.: 4.85

Accomplishments

Tied for Best of Show in regional competition, Technology Challenge '92, held at
Massachusetts Institute of Technology, for the design and construction of a
hovercraft.

Qualified for competition in Technology Challenge '91 with the design and
construction of a solar-powered remote-controlled sailboat.

Completed the following course work, maintaining a 6.0 grade average:
* Drafting 1 - 4   * Metal Technology
* Electricity/Electronics   * Wood Technology
* Computer-Aided Drafting   * Design & Technology 1 - 2
* Career Mechanics

Participated in Cooperative Work Experience projects in drafting and career
mechanics.

Work Experience

Drafting Intern, Cardell Associates, Baltimore, Maryland, Summer 1992
Duties: Checked blueprints of CAD-drafted plans for parts and equipment
manufactured by Cardell. Drafted initial drawings of existing parts that required
changes to fit new machinery.

Mechanics Intern, East Baltimore Auto, Summer 1991
Duties: Worked as assistant mechanic for import cars. Learned diagnostics
procedures and equipment operation.

Activities

Techies, CCHS technology club
Young Sailors of Baltimore
Radio Club

References and portfolio of drafting projects available on request.

Bruce C. Cantrell
120 Border Street
Hot Springs, Arkansas 71901
Telephone: 501/555-7367

OBJECTIVE

Summer internship with company doing business with international import and export trade.

EDUCATION

Lakeside Senior High School, Malvern Road, Hot Springs, Arkansas
Graduation date: 1992. Major: Business.

Specialized Courses: business series courses in accounting and management, marketing, Japanese I and II, economics, introduction to statistics. Current GPA: 3.9.

Special Projects: Developed three-year business finance, development and marketing plan for simulated business. In economics, made most significant profit margin from series of planned investments.

WORK EXPERIENCE

Garland County Exposition Center, Hot Springs, Arkansas.	Work Crew
Supervisor: Morgan Stewart.	October 1990 to present

Duties: Worked during summer exhibition season. Responsibilities included grounds maintenance, ticket selling, livestock herding and registration, and event preparation.

Sentinel-Record, Hot Springs, Arkansas.	Newspaper delivery
Supervisor: Walter E. Ballentine Jr.	September 1986 - May 1991

Lakeside Senior High School	Grounds Crew
Supervisor: Connie Lofstedt	August 1989

ACTIVITIES

Future Business Leaders of America, Hot Springs Junior Achievement, Junior Class Treasurer, S Club (service honorary).

References are available on request.

• **Brittany Schoonover** •
318 S.E. 151st • Eugene, Oregon 97405 • (503) 555-6246

Education

- South Eugene High School, Eugene, Oregon
  Expected graduation date: 1993

- Rex Putnam High School, 4950 S.E. Roethe Road, Milwaukie, Oregon 97267
  1989 - 1991

Skills

- Typing (55 wpm)
- Computer keyboarding (70 wpm)
- Ten-key adding machine (40 npm)

- Strong writing skills
- Business communications training
- Business systems training

Work Experience

- Data entry, State of Oregon Human Resources Division, Eugene, Oregon 97233
  June-August 1992

  Duties include transferring data from handwritten forms into computer forms, checking data entries for accuracy and making needed corrections, and sorting and filing computer printouts.

Activities

- Peer tutor in language arts
- Rally squad, junior varsity basketball
- Social events program committee
- Library assistance league
- School literary magazine editorial committee
- Hobbies include snow skiing, river rafting, singing, fiction writing, and reading

References

- Available on request.

Melinda W. Adams
810 N. 1430 Del Rio Drive
Tempe, Arizona 85282
(503) 555-9530

Objective

- Seeking summer employment in retail sales that will continue as part-time employment during the school year.

Education

- Corona Del Sol High School. Expected graduation date: 1994.
  - computer applications
  - word processing/typing
  - office management
  - two years of math
  - two years of business

Work Experience

- Office assistant, Dave Whitehead Insurance Company, Tempe. Sept. 1991 to present
  Duties include: answering telephones, assisting clients, answering questions about insurance claims, filling out claim forms, operating office machines, typing and filing.

- Cashier and Hostess, Judie's Chicken Haven, Lakeshore Drive, Tempe. June-Oct. 1991
  Duties included: greeting and seating customers, assisting waitresses and busboys with clearing and setting tables, entering sales in cash register, making change.

Achievements

- Volleyball and basketball team member; volleyball player of the year 1991
- First flute soloist, concert orchestra
- Jazz ensemble
- Drill team; served as captain 1991-92
- Music Appreciation Club member

References

- Available on request

KARIN BOWLES   2050 CROWN BOULEVARD, APT. C • DENVER, CO 80204 • (303) 555-2280

GOAL   A career in business administration.

EXPERIENCE

LEADERSHIP   As a member of the finance committee for the Associated Students of Kennedy High School, I was responsible for supervising the planning and execution of schoolwide fund-raising projects such as candy sales and the student carnival. I also set meeting dates and presided over meetings, reported to the student council, and worked with the student government advisor on budgeting.

COMMUNICATION   Worked on the publicity committees for several student events and election campaigns. Wrote text for fliers, signs, and assisted with speech writing. Each campaign ended in election victory for my candidate.

Completed two semesters of business communications courses. Also completed three years of honors-level English composition and three years of French. Have a working knowledge of spoken and written French.

ORGANIZATION   Served as assistant librarian, a position usually held by a paid professional, during the semester prior to graduation. Directed a research methods seminar for freshman students. Answered questions about library reference materials and card catalog filing systems. Supervised student workers in shelving books. Assisted with transfer of card catalog to computerized database.

EDUCATION   Kennedy High School
2855 S. Lamar Street
Denver, CO 80227
9/88 - 6/92
Final GPA: 3.75

Pertinent Courses: business law, accounting, computer applications in business, office procedures, word processing/typing, business management

REFERENCES   Available on request

Jennifer Smith   345 Forest Street, Dover, Delaware 19901
                                                                      (302) 555-5835

Job Sought

Classroom assistant position in preschool, day care center, or elementary school.

Relevant Experience

Dover Elementary School
Supervisor: Mrs. Wilkerson

Duties: Worked for one semester as part of exploratory education experience class. Assisted kindergarten teacher with supervision of students on playground and during classroom activities. Read stories and directed group activities. Taught songs and rhythm.

Education

9/89 – 6/93   Dover High School, Walker Road, Dover, Delaware

9/85 - 6/88   Dover Air Force Base Middle School, Hawthorne Drive, Dover, Delaware

Related Coursework:

Exploring childhood 1 and 2, human development, first aid and safety, basic health

Work History

6/91-present   Clerk, Dover AFB Commissary. Assist with stocking and display preparation.

References on request.

Judith Fritsch
16047 E. Bentsen, Apartment 25
Portland, Oregon 97233
(503) 555-5121

Objective   To obtain a part-time clerical job in a city or county government office where I can utilize my office management skills.

Skills

- Professional attitude
- 10-key adding machine
- Typing 60 wpm
- Word processing 75 wpm
- Filing

- Organized
- Reliable
- Responsible
- Self-starter
- Motivated for success

Education

I am currently a Senior at Central High School, Bay City, with an expected graduation date of June 1993.

Graduation seminar project: currently involved in preparing an in-depth report on business management systems and operations in city and county government offices.

Work Experience

Receptionist
Thrifty Auto Leasing, 456 Central Boulevard, Bay City
July 1990 - January 1992

Duties: Managed telephone switchboard, assisted clients, directed clients to appropriate department, typed letters, typed auto leasing forms, filed, assisted sales staff.

References available on request

<u>Kenneth Zimmerman</u>
Route 32, Box 2216
Central Valley, New York 10917
(914) 555-4481

<u>Objective</u>

A position with a political action organization working for
social improvement.

<u>Education</u>

Monroe-Woodbury High School, Central Valley, NY.
Anticipated graduation date: 1993.

<u>Skills & Achievements</u>

* Experienced with a variety of computer software and hardware,
  including Word and Works on Mac and IBM.

* Experienced with providing customer service.

* Trained in basic bookkeeping, invoicing, inventory, and payroll
  procedures.

* Effective leadership skills: served as vice president of
  associated students of Monroe-Woodbury High School, founder
  and president of Students for Global Awareness, director of
  one-act play for student drama presentation.

* Excellent writing and communications skills. Wrote and
  presented several speeches during all-school election
  campaign. Ran on platform of working to improve student
  awareness of global issues.

<u>Employment History</u>

Sales Assistant, Video Circle, Chester, NY. June-Sept. 1991.
  Duties: Provide assistance to customers in video sales and
  rental store. Worked with database on IBM-compatible computer
  system. Handled cash and credit card transactions. Maintained
  accurate inventory system.

References available on request.

Mary Jo Azukas
14 West 22nd St.
Trenton, NJ 08602
(609) 555-3477

Objective

To obtain a position as assistant manager in a small restaurant.

Experience

Head Cashier, <u>Burgerville USA</u>., Trenton, Sept. 1991 - present

<u>Duties:</u> Supervise cashier staff during evening shift. Check balance sheets at end of shift. Work counter and drive-through window as needed.

Line Cashier/Cook, <u>Tony's Burger Emporium</u>, Trenton, June 1990 - Aug. 1991.

<u>Duties:</u> Greeted customers, took orders, helped kitchen crew prepare meals and drinks, assisted with maintaining stock, cleaning, and closing procedures. Responsible for having balanced till after each shift.

Education

Capitol High School, Trenton
Class of 1994

Honors

Cashier of the Month, <u>Burgerville</u>, February 1992
Junior Cheerleader of the Year, 1992
"Cappy" Award for best supporting actress in a student production, 1991

References are available on request.

ANTOINETTE RUPERT
238 Orange Street
Tampa, FL 33606
(813) 555-3953

OBJECTIVE

To become part of the support services team for a small but growing business.

EDUCATION

Tampa Central High School, 480 Sherman Parkway, New Haven. Diploma, June 1992.

Concentration: Accounting I and II, Computer Applications I and II (word processing, spreadsheet, database, design, page layout and communications software for MS DOS operating platforms), Business Management, and Business Communications.

EXPERIENCE

Temporary Clerical Worker. Kelly Services, 1991 - present.

Duties: Worked for a wide range of clients, including a bank, mortgage trust company, supply warehouse, architectural office, city government office, and law office. Duties included typing, filing, answering telephones, preparing forms, computer data entry, transcribing dictation, and general office assistance.

ACTIVITIES & ACHIEVEMENTS

Secretary, Junior Class TCHS, 1991-1992
Assistant Editor, TCHS Yearbook, 1990-1991
Secretary, Future Business Leaders of America, 1989-1990
Member, Student Recycling Committee, 1991-1992
Participant, Girls' State, 1991
Member, TCHS Camera Club, 1990-1992

References are available on request

PAUL JEROME
412 Lincoln
Las Vegas, Nevada 87701
505-555-6623

OBJECTIVE: Seeking summer employment on the restaurant staff of a large hotel. Long-term goal: a career in hotel and restaurant management.

EDUCATION:
- South High School, 300 Chesterfield Avenue, Las Vegas Class of 1993.

EXPERIENCE: Grounds Crew, Circus Circus, Las Vegas. June-August 1992.

- Duties: Trimmed hedges, replaced indoor and outdoor plants, operated irrigation system, kept walkways and grounds clean, assisted with pool maintenance.

Busboy, Denny's Restaurant, Las Vegas. September 1991-present.

- Duties: Assist waitresses with serving meals, clear and set tables, serve water, coffee, and other drinks.

Maintenance Crew, Caesar's Palace, Las Vegas. June-August 1991.

- Duties: Maintained regular schedule of pool maintenance, assisted with janitorial responsibilities, worked with grounds crew on landscape maintenance, provided some assistance with equipment repair.

INTERESTS:
- Gourmet cooking, swimming team, archery, tennis.

References are available on request.

Tony Pomeroy
2307 N. Broad Street
Philadelphia, PA 19119
(215) 555-2258

OBJECTIVE

A staff position as a photographer or darkroom technician on a newspaper or magazine.

EDUCATION

Northeast Prep School, Cottman Avenue, Philadelphia. Class of 1992.

Course emphases: Journalism, Photojournalism, Photography 1-3, Darkroom (beginning and advanced), Computer Applications in Art

RELEVANT SKILLS & EXPERIENCE

Completed projects in three fields: black and white 35 mm photography, photo silkscreen and offset printing, and computer alteration of photographic imagery (using Digital Darkroom on Macintosh computer).

Won first place in *Philadelphia Daily News* amateur photo contest, high school category. Photo published in July 1992 edition.

Completed photo essay for submission to regional amateur photo contest sponsored by Kodak. (Results as yet undetermined.)

Operated copy camera for making PMTs and halftone screens.

Completed extracurricular project on 35mm color photography.

WORK HISTORY

Northeast Prep Student Newspaper
Photo Editor, September 1991-92
Staff Photographer, September 1988-92

Supervised student photography staff. Selected photographs for publication from analysis of negatives or contact sheets. Assigned photography projects and maintained check-out of school cameras. Shot, developed, and printed photographs.

EXTRACURRICULAR ACTIVITIES

Camera Club, president
Brush and Easel (art students association)

PORTFOLIO AND REFERENCES AVAILABLE UPON REQUEST

Timothy J. Davison
1286 West Shore Road, Apt. 5
Warwick, Rhode Island 02889
Telephone: 555-2117

Objective

A position as chef's assistant at a restaurant featuring specialty or gourmet cuisine.

Education

The Culinary Institute
114 Fifth Avenue
New York, NY 10019
Video correspondence course, to be completed December 1992

Tollgate Senior High School
575 Centerville Road
Warwick, RI 02886
Class standing: Junior

Special Skills

* Worked with International Student Club to plan and prepare a meal for 250 parents and students. Involved with menu planning and food preparation for dishes from all over the world.

* Catered a dinner party for six people as part of a donation of services to fund-raise for the local Boys and Girls Club. Prepared and helped serve five-course dinner.

* Completed one year of culinary video correspondence course that involved preparation of primarily French cuisine. Although not required by the course, I have followed a procedure of preparing the lesson plan menu for a group of four to six people who provide a written evaluation of the meal and its presentation.

* Completed two years of high school food preparation courses, including experience with food decoration.

* Worked on prep station in kitchen of gourmet restaurant. Assisted with first-stage food preparation.

Work Experience

Kitchen Prep Staff, June 1991-present
Warwick Towers Restaurant
34 Warwick Lake Avenue
Warwick, RI 02889

References are available on request.

Toby Waterson
200 South Third Avenue
Arcadia, California 91006
213-555-9226

Objective	To obtain a job with the technical department of a manufacturing company.
Experience	**Technical Design**

Technical Design
- Designed and built solar-powered car (one-person).
- Designed multi-media computer-directed light and sound presentation.
- Developed model for automated, solar-powered home.
- Completed two years of design and technology program.

Engine Mechanics
- Built motor for solar-powered car.
- Assisted with engine rebuilding on two Volkswagens.
- Assisted in engine repair on riding and other lawn mowers.

Work History

Grounds Crew/Maintenance, June 1991-
Riverview Apartments
Arcadia, California

- Duties: landscape maintenance; some plumbing, carpentry, general repair.

Library Assistant, 1990-1991
Foothills Junior High School
Arcadia, California

- Duties: audio-visual equipment repair, office work, reshelving, data entry.

Education

Arcadia Senior High School, Class of 1992
Major: Design and Technology

References

Available on request

Jasmine Parker
4223 Kilauea Avenue
P.O. Box 2214
Honolulu, Hawaii 96819
Phone: 555-2294

Objective

To obtain a position in fisheries and wildlife administration that will utilize my skills in scientific research, analysis, and communication.

Education

Honolulu Community College, Dillingham Boulevard.
Enrolled in summer open enrollment programs, 1991 and 1992.
Earned 3.6 GPA in science courses.

Kaimuki High School, 2705 Kaimuki Avenue, Honolulu.
Graduated 1992. Science GPA, 4.0. Cumulative GPA, 3.56.

Science Background

Designed and conducted research project on underwater testing procedures.
Assisted with research project designed to decrease mercury toxicity.
Completed two years of general biology, including one college-level course.
Completed two semesters of marine biology, including one college-level course.
Completed one college-level course in scientific research methods.
Completed one college-level course in fisheries science.

Communications Background

Wrote report on fisheries management problems in Hawaii, presented at Science '91.
Completed four years of writing, including college-level course in technical writing.
Member, Kaimuki High School Forensics Club; presented several prepared speeches.
Winner, Honolulu Toastmasters Honorable Mention for presentation on science careers for women.

References

Available upon request.

▲ **Sandra G. Naylor**
1415 NE San Rafael Street
Santa Cruz, California 95061
Telephone: 555-0439

▲ **Education**

1989 - present: Santa Cruz Senior High School

1979-1985: Alvore School of Dance, San Francisco

▲ **Experience**

Part-time receptionist, Dr. Jonothan Naylor, Santa Cruz, 1989-present

Duties include answering telephones, calling patients to remind them about appointments, scheduling appointments, checking patients in, assisting with billing to insurance companies and patients, typing, and filing.

▲ **Skills**

Experienced with office reception desk responsibilities.
Typing 50 w.p.m. on electric typewriter; 75 w.p.m. on computer word processing (Word Perfect).
Shorthand 90 w.p.m.
Experienced with mail merge capabilities of computer word processing.
Pleasant telephone manner.

▲ **Activities**

Chair, Winterfest committee
Homecoming committee member
Dance team
School musicals and plays
Softball team

▲ **References**

Available upon request.

Brandon Reaman

1147 N.E. 160th   Telephone: 555-1361
Portland, Oregon 97230

Objective

Summer employment with construction crew.

Experience and Skills

My work experience includes assisting with roofing, building fences, and providing lawn and garden maintenance. I have worked for a private contractor to build a deck, remodel a kitchen, and reconstruct an 18x24-foot front porch that had collapsed.

In design and technology program, worked with a team of three other students to design and build a balsa wood bridge that could support at least 50 pounds. Our design exceeded 100.

Able to operate the following: lathe, table saw, drill press, compression hammer, and other metal and woodworking machinery.

Work History

Crew member, Red Hat Remodeling, June-September 1991

Crew member, Johnson Construction, June-September 1990

Education

Reynolds High School, 1698 S.W. Cherry Park Road, Troutdale, Oregon 97060
Expected graduation date: 1993

Relevant Coursework

Practical Physics, Woods II, Metals II, Building Construction, Design and Technology

References

Available upon request

SHARON ANNE GILBERT
1735 N.E. Moore
Chattanooga, Tennessee 37402
Telephone: 615/555-3374

EDUCATION

Howard High School, 2500 S. Market Street, Chattanooga
    Graduation date: 1993. Major: Business.

SKILLS

Typing, filing, organizing. Able to operate the following: IBM and Macintosh computers
    (various word processing programs), ten-key adding machine, postage meter. Have valid
    driver's license.

WORK EXPERIENCE

Child care provider. Mrs. Jolie Chappell (full-time summers) and various other families (part-
    time throughout the year). 1988 - present.

    Provide care for children of various ages. Responsible for feeding and observing nap time
    and bedtime routines. I am always careful to leave the house as I found it and to help the
    children learn a sense of responsibility about their environment.

ACTIVITIES

Church choir and youth group
Howard High Concert Choir
Social Committee
Publicity Committee (Student Government)
One year Symphony Orchestra

REFERENCES

Available on request

STEPHEN P. DILLON
18445 S.W. Mirick Road
Denton, Texas 76201
817-555-4550

JOB OBJECTIVE

To secure a position on a carpentry crew for full-time summer employment.

EDUCATION

Denton Senior High School, 1007 Fulton Street, Denton
Graduation date: 1993

Related courses of study: Home building construction (PGE Good Sense Home), wood shop I and II, auto technology. Maintained top grades in each of these courses.

WORK EXPERIENCE

Worker for Buzz Burton (private contractor), Aug. 1991-present, as work is available.
Completed deck construction project, washed and painted interior and exterior of buildings, built foundation forms. Assisted with framing and roofing.

Andersen Construction, September 1991.
Stripped and refitted a kitchen according to code specifications; installed insulation; removed and replanted shrubbery.

Excavation Crew Member, Morse Brothers Concrete, summers during 1990 and 1991.
Worked on ditch digging crew. Operated chain saw, jumping jack, trencher, backhoe, cat loader, and dump truck.

ACTIVITIES

Four years wrestling, two years football, assistant coach for girls' softball.

References available upon request.

RAYMOND KELLER
1709 S.29th
Sheboygan, Wisconsin 53082
Telephone: 414-555-1665

OBJECTIVE

Obtain position as apprentice mechanic in auto repair center.

EDUCATION

North High School, Sheboygan, Wisconsin 53081
Expected graduation date: 1993

COURSES TAKEN

Auto Mechanics 1-2
Career Mechanics
Principles of Technology
Metal Shop
Wood Shop
Design & Technology
Drafting
Electricity/Electronics

WORK EXPERIENCE

Shop Steward, Sheboygan North Auto Shop, 1991-present
(Student-run auto center located at high school; run diagnostics, estimate costs, supervise
repairs.)

Station Attendant, Winnebago Garage, S. 17th Street, Sheboygan, Wisconsin, August 1990-
present

Station Attendant, Four Towers Shell, S. 13th Street, Sheboygan, Wisconsin, 1989-1990

ACTIVITIES

Four years high school football, Letterman's Club, boating and fishing

References are available on request.

JERIANNE JONES
1288 N.W. 58th Avenue
Seattle, Washington 98117
Telephone: 206/555-1941

EDUCATION

Ballard High School. Expected graduation date: 1993.

Lakeside Upper School, Seattle. Attended 1989-91.

EXPERIENCE

Clerical:
During the school year I work in the school's central office as a clerical assistant. My responsibilities include typing, operating various duplication machines for the teachers and secretaries, filing, and delivering messages. I received consistently high reviews for each of the two years I served as an assistant.

Counseling:
In May 1990 and April 1991, I served as a counselor at the Bainbridge Island Outdoor School. I supervised the children on the buses and took them on discovery walks through the rain forest.

In the summers of 1989 and 1990 I spent several weeks as a YWCA camp counselor, teaching outdoor survival skills, canoeing, and swimming. I hold an up-to-date advanced life saving certificate.

Volunteer:
As a member of the student welfare committee, I planned a social awareness week which brought speakers from several Seattle social service agencies to speak at the high school. I organized food and clothing drive at Ballard High School for relief following earthquakes in Nicaragua and worked with a charitable organization to raise money for Romanian orphans.

ACHIEVEMENTS
Selected to present student essay on volunteerism at Lyons Club, Ballard Chapter
Worked on student yearbook staff as copy editor
Member of ASBHS student welfare committee

REFERENCES
Available on request

JORY AHRENS
131 - 172nd Avenue N.E.
Bellevue, Washington 98006
Telephone: (206) 555-9027

OBJECTIVE

To obtain a retail sales position in a women's clothing department or boutique. My long-range objective is a career in fashion merchandising.

EDUCATION

Sammamish High School, 469 - 148th S.W., Bellevue
Expected graduation date: 1993

WORK EXPERIENCE

Student Manager   SHS Athletics Shop, Sammamish High School, 1991 to 1992.
Worked with committee to select and purchase merchandise for student-run sports shop, which carries t-shirts and sweatshirts, rental equipment, and sporting goods. Supervised student workers, applied transfer designs to clothing, and oversaw budgeting and finance committee.

Sales
Representative   Earrings Galore, Mall 205, November 1988 to October 1991.
Served customers, made sales, and operated the cash register. I also assisted with preparing window displays.

SKILLS

Experienced with operating a cash register, Macintosh computer, scientific calculator, and typewriter (45 wpm).

ACTIVITIES

Served as a counselor at Outdoor School. Member of International Club. Played three years of team volleyball. Work at school track meets.

REFERENCES   Available upon request.

Chapter Six

SAMPLE COVER LETTERS

16825 N.E. Clarkston
Battle Creek, MI 49017
September 21, 1992

Sales Manager
Robnett's Hardware
2260 N.E. Delaney
Battle Creek, MI 49014

Enclosed please find my resume, submitted in response to your advertisement for a sales clerk in Sunday's edition of the <u>Battle Creek Enquirer</u>.

I was most recently employed with Battle Creek Auto Parts, but the owner retired and closed the store, and I am eager to continue working in the field of retail sales. I have had experience with auto mechanics, woodworking, metalworking, and electronics, and am therefore familiar with your product line. I have also helped my father with home maintenance and repair projects.

I look forward to having an opportunity to discuss my qualifications with you. My telephone number is 555-3420, and I am available after 2:30 p.m. daily. Thank you for your consideration.

Sincerely,

Janine Hartney

• **Juan Aguilar** •

September 1, 1992

Charles Hansen
Production Manager
The Herald-Palladium
3450 Hollywood Road
St. Joseph, MI 49085

Dear Mr. Hansen:

Mr. George Petersen of Michigan Printing suggested I contact you with regard to my enthusiastic interest in a career in the printing industry. I would like to apply for a position as an apprentice printer and have enclosed my resume for your consideration.

This past summer I worked for Mr. Petersen as a print shop assistant. As the summer vacation relief worker, I was able to move throughout the printing department, and in the process I learned a tremendous amount about the trade. In addition, my course work in graphic arts and computer applications has given me a background that will be very useful as the printing industry gets more involved in electronic pre-press.

I would very much appreciate an opportunity to come by to talk with you and see the printing operations at the newspaper. Mr. Petersen spoke very highly of the production department, and I hope to become part of your team. I will call you within the next few days, or you may reach me at the number below most afternoons.

Sincerely,

Juan Aguilar

• **158 Halladay S.W.** • **Benton Harbor, MI 49028** • **(616) 555-7379** •

990 Woody Road
Dallas, Texas 75253
15 May 1992

Anita Blakeley
Manager
Blakeley Distributors
886 Denton Road
Dallas, Texas 75259

Dear Ms. Blakeley:

I would like to apply for the position of assistant manager advertised in the May 9 edition of the <u>Times Herald</u>.

As indicated in the enclosed resume, I have had some previous managerial experience. At Taco Time my duties frequently included taking over full responsibility for restaurant operations in the absence of the manager. I became adept at dealing with a variety of crises, from finding substitutes for workers who failed to report to work during rush hour, to dealing successfully with surprise inspections from the health and fire departments.

As a recent high school graduate, I may seem young, but I would like to emphasize my commitment to a long-term relationship with Blakeley Distributors. I would like to use my organizational skills, business training, and interpersonal skills to serve your company to the best of my ability.

I hope to have an opportunity to talk with you at your convenience about my experiences and training and how they qualify me for the job. My telephone number is 555-2369, and I am available most mornings.

Thank you for your consideration.

Sincerely,

Brian McGavin

Kendra Wallen
1137 N.E. 189th • Provo, Utah 84604 • (801) 555-2740

March 11, 1992

Sandra Mason
Director
YWCA Lakeside Camp
22 Lakeshore Road
Provo, Utah 84612

Dear Ms. Mason:

I would like to submit my resume for your consideration in selecting teachers for this summer's camp programs. Having attended camp as an elementary school student for several years, I am familiar with the program and believe I have a lot to contribute toward making the summer camp experience memorable for others.

My concentration in high school has been art, and I have used my training and love of all art media to develop projects that would be fun and rewarding for children, from pre-school age through sixth grade. Projects have included paper and fabric marbling, tie-dying t-shirts, making pottery beads, and making natural dyes from leaves, roots, and other items gathered on nature walks.

I would like to show you the results of some of these projects and discuss my qualifications with you further. Please call me at your convenience. I can be reached at the number above in the afternoons, or you may leave a message and I will return your call promptly. Thank you very much for considering my application.

Yours truly,

Kendra Wallen

September 20, 1992

Mr. Henry B. Thurston
Assistant to the Director
Washington Children's Services Division
220 W. First
Seattle, WA 98022

Dear Mr. Thurston:

I am writing to apply for an internship with the Washington Children's Services Division. I understand from my child development instructor, Susan Bishop, that you have four such positions available each summer.

My educational training in child development and psychology have already been beneficial in programs I have been involved with. I have become especially interested in carrying anti-drug and alcohol messages to young people. Toward this end, I worked with the Boys and Girls Club of South Seattle and started a club at Tyee High School, "Tyee (Naturally) High Club," which has stirred a tremendous response among students.

I will be happy to serve CSD in whatever capacity I may be most useful. I have a variety of skills in addition to those listed on my resume. Specifically, I am familiar with computer word processing and am quite capable at general clerical work. I would like to speak with you at your convenience about your expectations for the student intern and how I might best contribute to CSD's efforts. My telephone number is 555-9225, and I am available in the early morning and afternoon.

Sincerely,

Jason Raintree
2268-A S. 187th Street
Seattle, WA 98055

2250 Collis Avenue
Huntington, WV 25702
June 26, 1992

Mr. Frank Westerman
Fire Chief
Huntington Fire District
680 Temple Avenue
Huntington, WV 25702

Dear Mr. Westerman:

I was delighted to see your advertisement for firefighter
trainees in yesterday's Herald-Dispatch because it has been my
lifelong ambition to become a firefighter. Enclosed is my
resume for your review.

My activities and course work in high school have centered
around health, physical fitness, and sports. I have maintained
excellent physical condition, which your advertisement
indicates is a must for potential firefighters. I have also
had advanced training in first aid and CPR.

Once you have had an opportunity to review my resume, I will
call to set up an appointment at your convenience to further
discuss my interests and qualifications. I am eager to pursue
a career in fire prevention and protection.

Sincerely,

Robert Goldstein

May 15, 1992

J. E. Davis
Stanton Electronics
2516 West Palm Drive, Suite 116
Laguna Beach, CA 92653

Dear J.E. Davis:

In reply to your recent advertisement in the _Times_, I have enclosed my resume for consideration in the search for an electronics technician.

I believe my training and experience provide me with the background you are looking for. My work in the design and manufacturing of radar-controlled devices will allow me to immediately take on challenges for Stanton Electronics.

I look forward to having an opportunity to visit your facilities and talk with you about the projects I have completed. I will be happy to bring some of the more relevant of these in order for you to see the quality of my work and the innovation in the designs. My number is (213) 555-9562, and I may be reached most mornings.

Thank you for your consideration.

Sincerely,

Masoud Ysmiri
211 South Grevillea Avenue
Apt. 26B
Inglewood, CA 90301

3836 Sweetwater Avenue
Scottsdale, AZ 85254
May 6, 1992

Carol Emory
Emory & Associates
One West Monroe
Suite 2017
Phoenix, AZ 85004

Dear Ms. Emory:

I am writing to request the opportunity to work for you as a
summer intern. I understand from my adviser at Stanford that
your firm often takes on student interns.

I will graduate from Chaparral High School in Scottsdale this
month, and will enter Stanford University's pre-law program in
September. I hope to use my summer to learn more about private
legal practice by working in whatever way I might best
contribute to your firm.

As the enclosed resume may indicate, I am a hard worker who
takes pride in doing the best possible job at whatever task I
take on. I hold a 4.0 grade point average, and will graduate
in the top five percent of my class. I have experience in
research and clerical work, and I am willing to put in the
long hours that are standard for anyone involved in legal
practice.

I would like to arrange a time to visit with you at your
convenience to learn more about how I can contribute my
abilities. My telephone number is (602) 555-2834 and I am
available after 3:30 daily.

Yours sincerely,

Paul Garcia

435 South Monaco Parkway
Denver, CO 80204
February 15, 1992

Mr. John Seward
Seward and Whitely, CPAs
21 West Riddlington
Denver, CO 80216

Dear Mr. Seward:

I am responding to the February 10 advertisement in the Post announcing openings for part-time temporary accounting clerks. Enclosed is my resume for your review.

As my resume indicates, I have received extensive training in accounting and bookkeeping and am familiar with several computer software programs that deal with accounting. Working for your company will be a timely opportunity to put these skills to the challenge of aiding your firm during the tax season. Upon graduation, I hope to pursue a college degree in accounting.

I would appreciate an opportunity to meet with you, at your convenience, to discuss the position. The advertisement indicated that hours were flexible, and as I am still in school, I would be available to work any day after 2:00 p.m. and could extend my hours as long as necessary to accomplish the job. I may be reached at 555-4481 any afternoon. Thank you for your consideration, and I look forward to talking with you.

Sincerely,

Michael Han

128 Orange Street
New Haven, CT 06510
April 26, 1992

Verna Howard
Office Manager
Benson, Keller, Harcourt, and Vinson, Attorneys at Law
Twelve Front Avenue
Suite 1200
New Haven, CT 06508

Dear Ms. Howard:

Enclosed please find a resume and letters of recommendation, submitted in response to your recent advertisement for a paralegal assistant.

I will graduate with highest honors from Hillhouse High School next month following a four-year curriculum centered on business, law, and office management. I believe my training and my previous experience as an office assistant in the firm of Switter, Harvey, Jenkins, & Hewitt, have prepared me for assuming the responsibilities of a paralegal assistant.

I would appreciate the opportunity to meet with you at your convenience. I am eager to put my skills to work for your firm. I may be reached at 555-3754 in the afternoons. Thank you for considering my application.

Yours truly,

Judy Reimer

2240 Nebraska Ave. N.W.
Washington, D.C. 20016
May 28, 1992

Mrs. Belinda Summers
Director
Jefferson Montessori School
620 Jefferson Ave. N.W.
Washington, D.C. 20018

Dear Mrs. Summers:

I would like to put forward my application for a summer program guide position at Jefferson Montessori, advertised in the *City Paper*.

I was a Montessori child myself, through eighth grade, and am both familiar with and appreciative of the program's philosophy. My experiences as a day camp leader and outdoor school counselor have firmed my resolve to enter a career in early childhood education. I believe my background in Montessori as well as my training and experiences in working with children enable me to offer a worthwhile contribution to your school.

In addition, as a Native American I have taken special efforts to learn the history, crafts, songs, and dances of my heritage. By teaching songs, stories, and crafts I am able to share with others the richness of Native culture. I have had experience directing such activities with children of various ages.

I would like to visit the school and talk with you at your convenience. I am available any afternoon and can be reached at 555-7465. Thank you for your consideration. I look forward to talking with you.

Sincerely,

Mary Jo Baptiste

Claire Renard   618 N.W. Eighth Street, No. 215
                                            Boca Raton, Florida 33486
                                            Telephone: 555-1400

May 12, 1992

Mr. Harold Washington
Assistant Manager
Florida State Bank
224 N.W. Fifth Street
Boca Raton, FL 33486

Dear Mr. Washington:

I am writing in response to your May 6 advertisement for bank tellers. Enclosed you will find my resume and two letters of recommendation for your review.

As indicated in my resume, the focus of my course work has been business and accounting. My experiences as treasurer of the student body and on the school's student finance committee have provided an excellent opportunity for me to exercise the skills learned in the classroom. I was responsible for managing the budget for the entire student body, authorizing disbursements, developing a financial plan for the year, and providing monthly financial reports.

I would like to arrange an interview at your convenience so that I may learn more about your expectations for prospective tellers. I believe I can assure you that I will meet your qualifications. I may be reached at the above number in the afternoons, and any time after May 21st. Thank you for your consideration.

Yours truly,

Claire Renard

Laura Chen
5527 N.W. Oak Creek Road
Ashland, Oregon 97520
(503) 555-9882

18 May 1992

Everard Carlisle
Director
Sierra Club International
Central Office
358 Geary
San Francisco, CA 94101

Dear Mr. Carlisle:

The position announced in the May 2 <u>Chronicle</u> appears to be the perfect opportunity to put my skills in science and business, together with my abiding interest in the environment, to work for the betterment of the earth. Enclosed please find my resume, submitted in application for the entry-level position in your research and economics division.

As my resume indicates, I have an extensive background in the earth and natural sciences, as well as a strong record in business and economics courses. Capstone economics, in particular, was a challenging course that allowed students the opportunity to unravel economic mysteries by learning and practicing careful economic reasoning in analysis of particular economic situations. I chose as my topic of endeavor to anticipate and evaluate the impact of the savings and loan crisis on federal environmental programs. It was a fascinating project, and I would enjoy having an opportunity to share the findings with you.

I am planning a trip to the Bay Area early next month and would like to visit with you at that time, if possible. The dates of my trip are not yet settled, so I can arrange my schedule to your convenience. Please write to me at the above address, or call me at (503) 555-9982. I look forward to speaking with you.

Sincerely,

Laura Chen

May 26, 1992

Ms. Elaine Richardson
Personnel Director
Microsoft Corporation
226 Industrial Way
Everett, WA 98203

Dear Ms. Richardson:

I would like to submit my resume in application for an entry-level position in the research and development department. I will be attending the University of Washington in Seattle this fall in computer programming, and I believe my experience and training thus far will enable me to be an asset to Microsoft.

My high school computer teacher, Mr. Earl Phillips, is a gifted computer scientist, and it has been a great privilege to study with him. He has challenged my own innate interest and ability in computer programming and technology to push my ideas toward greater and greater innovation. I have tackled programming problems in BASIC, PASCAL, FORTRAN, and Hypercard environments, working on DOS, Macintosh, and UNIX platforms.

I would appreciate an opportunity to meet with you and the director of research and development and share the results of my own programming efforts. I will be moving to the Seattle area within the next week and will contact you shortly thereafter. I look forward to seeing the Microsoft operation firsthand.

Thank you for your consideration.

Sincerely,

Dylan J. McDonald
1415 Wenig Road N.E.
Cedar Rapids, IA 52402

2248 W. Billtown Road, Apt. 16
Louisville, KY 40215
Telephone: 502/555-7751

June 3, 1992

Ms. Teresa Valdez
Staff Nurse
Louisville Care Center
16815 W. MacKay
Louisville, KY 40215

Dear Ms. Valdez:

I would like to submit my resume to you in application for a position as nurse's aide at the Louisville Care Center. I spoke with your assistant, Jenna Bradley, who indicated that there were two such positions available and that I should write to you directly.

My experiences as a candy striper at Louisville General have prepared me for the realization that working in a health care facility is often very tough, both physically and emotionally. I believe, however, that I am equal to the challenge, and I would very much like to make a contribution to the caring environment at the Louisville Care Center.

I would like to come in and speak with you about my qualifications and how I can best fulfill your expectations for this position. I look forward to hearing from you. I am available at the above number most mornings. Thank you for your consideration.

Yours truly,

Suzanne Barstow

May 22, 1992

Bradford Williamson
Personnel Director
Electronics Enterprises
1810 S. Olive
Los Angeles, California 90015

Dear Mr. Williamson:

I am writing in reply to your advertisement in the Sunday Times for technicians. Please accept my resume in application for the position.

I have two years of classroom training in design and technology, a program designed to allow students to define and solve their own technological design problems. I have also had course work in electronics, engine mechanics, and computer-assisted drafting. Two of the projects I developed in these courses—a solar-powered car and a computer-directed light and sound presentation—have been submitted to national competition.

I would appreciate receiving an opportunity to meet with you and discuss my qualifications for the position of technician. I may be reached at (213) 555-9226 in the afternoons, and will arrange to meet at your convenience. Thank you for considering my application.

Sincerely yours,

Toby Waterson
200 South Third Avenue
Arcadia, CA 91006

3320 Delaware Avenue
Buffalo, New York 14222
May 18, 1992

Susan Simonson
Manager
Musicland
128 North Seventh
Buffalo, New York 14225

Dear Ms. Simonson:

In reply to your advertisement in the Buffalo News of May 16, I am enclosing my resume to apply for the position of evening sales clerk.

I have had a deep and abiding interest in music for many years, and have received formal training in both classical and jazz singing. My listening interests in music are much broader, and I keep up-to-date on contemporary musicians from rap to rock.

I would like to set up a time at your convenience to come by the store and talk with you about the position. I am currently working as a singing hostess, but would enjoy an opportunity to work in retail sales for a company involved with music. I can be reached at 555-2193 after 3:30 most afternoons. Thank you for the opportunity to apply.

Sincerely,

Michelle M. Hibbard

412 Lincoln
Las Vegas, NV 87701

May 22, 1992

Mr. Eric Swensen
Personnel Director
The Mirage
Las Vegas, NV 87702

Dear Mr. Swensen:

I am writing to apply for a position with one of The Mirage's restaurants. I am interested in serving as a waiter, busboy, or kitchen assistant. John Rivers at Circus Circus suggested I write to you concerning the availability of summer employment.

I worked for Mr. Rivers last summer, and though he was pleased with my work, I would prefer to gain more experience in the restaurant area of hotel operations. I am currently working at Denny's, but am eager to return to a hotel environment. I plan to continue my education in hotel and restaurant management.

I would appreciate an opportunity to talk with you about summer employment opportunities at The Mirage. I have long admired the hotel and would enjoy doing my best to serve your restaurant guests. Please call me at 555-6623 at your convenience.

Thank you for your consideration.

Sincerely,

Paul Jerome

2240 W. Yucca Street
Santa Fe, New Mexico 87538
May 20, 1992

Personnel Director
Bellande Enterprises, Inc.
305 E. 102nd
Santa Fe, New Mexico 87536

Dear Director:

Today my accounting teacher, Ms. Cheryl Cooper, informed the class about several local job openings in the business field. The secretarial position with your company got my immediate attention. I would like to apply for this opening and have enclosed my resume for your consideration.

I have held two summer secretarial positions, which provided me with excellent clerical experience. My tasks included word processing and typing, managing a six-line telephone switchboard, operating a ten-key adding machine, as well as light bookkeeping and data input. My specialized courses in business operations and accounting have given me the specific skills needed to take on the challenges of a secretarial position. I am very responsible and organized, and I believe I will be an asset to your company.

Thank you for taking the time to review my resume. I would enjoy working for Bellande and would appreciate the opportunity to talk with you at your convenience. I may be reached after 3:00 p.m. at 555-5121.

Sincerely,

Maurya Angelino

Shelley Tabor

---

78 N.E. Towbridge
Bridgewater, MA 02324

26 May 1992

Ms. Paula Marshall
Director
Little Wonder Day Care
26 W. Fifth Avenue
Bridgewater, MA 02326

Dear Ms. Marshall:

I am writing in response to your advertisement for a part-time teaching assistant at Little Wonder Day Care. Enclosed is my resume for your consideration.

I have been involved with young children for as long as I can remember. I have four younger siblings, ranging in age from fifteen to three years of age. As the eldest, I was often responsible for watching over them.

For the past five years I have provided child care for two different families, including two summers of full-time care for three children. I always work hard at maintaining a happy, supportive environment, often bringing books and various art or music projects to share with the children. I never rely on television as a substitute for supervision.

I have received formalized training in childhood development and education from school courses and experience with the in-school day care center/preschool. The Preschool Practicum, one semester working half-days in the day care center, was an exceptional experience that convinced me to pursue a career in early childhood education.

I would like to come and talk with you further about the position and my qualifications. I am available most mornings at 555-8281. Thank you for your consideration.

                    Yours truly,

                    Shelley Tabor

VGM CAREER BOOKS

OPPORTUNITIES IN
Available in both paperback and hardbound editions

Accounting
Acting
Advertising
Aerospace
Agriculture
Airline
Animal and Pet Care
Architecture
Automotive Service
Banking
Beauty Culture
Biological Sciences
Biotechnology
Book Publishing
Broadcasting
Building Construction Trades
Business Communication
Business Management
Cable Television
Carpentry
Chemical Engineering
Chemistry
Child Care
Chiropractic Health Care
Civil Engineering
Cleaning Service
Commercial Art and Graphic Design
Computer Aided Design and Computer Aided Mfg.
Computer Maintenance
Computer Science
Counseling & Development
Crafts
Culinary
Customer Service
Dance
Data Processing
Dental Care
Direct Marketing
Drafting
Electrical Trades
Electronic and Electrical Engineering
Electronics
Energy
Engineering
Engineering Technology
Environmental
Eye Care
Fashion
Fast Food
Federal Government
Film
Financial
Fire Protection Services
Fitness
Food Services
Foreign Language
Forestry
Gerontology
Government Service
Graphic Communications
Health and Medical
High Tech
Home Economics
Hospital Administration
Hotel & Motel Management
Human Resources Management Careers
Information Systems
Insurance
Interior Design
International Business
Journalism
Laser Technology
Law

Law Enforcement and Criminal Justice
Library and Information Science
Machine Trades
Magazine Publishing
Management
Marine & Maritime
Marketing
Materials Science
Mechanical Engineering
Medical Technology
Metalworking
Microelectronics
Military
Modeling
Music
Newspaper Publishing
Nursing
Nutrition
Occupational Therapy
Office Occupations
Opticianry
Optometry
Packaging Science
Paralegal Careers
Paramedical Careers
Part-time & Summer Jobs
Performing Arts
Petroleum
Pharmacy
Photography
Physical Therapy
Physician
Plastics
Plumbing & Pipe Fitting
Podiatric Medicine
Postal Service
Printing
Property Management
Psychiatry
Psychology
Public Health
Public Relations
Purchasing
Real Estate
Recreation and Leisure
Refrigeration and Air Conditioning
Religious Service
Restaurant
Retailing
Robotics
Sales
Sales & Marketing
Secretarial
Securities
Social Science
Social Work
Speech-Language Pathology
Sports & Athletics
Sports Medicine
State and Local Government
Teaching
Technical Communications
Telecommunications
Television and Video
Theatrical Design & Production
Transportation
Travel
Trucking
Veterinary Medicine
Visual Arts
Vocational and Technical
Warehousing
Waste Management
Welding
Word Processing
Writing
Your Own Service Business

CAREERS IN
Accounting; Advertising; Business; Communications; Computers; Education; Engineering; Health Care; High Tech; Law; Marketing; Medicine; Science

CAREER DIRECTORIES
Careers Encyclopedia
Dictionary of Occupational Titles
Occupational Outlook Handbook

CAREER PLANNING
Admissions Guide to Selective Business Schools
Career Planning and Development for College Students and Recent Graduates
Careers Checklists
Careers for Animal Lovers
Careers for Bookworms
Careers for Culture Lovers
Careers for Foreign Language Aficionados
Careers for Good Samaritans
Careers for Gourmets
Careers for Nature Lovers
Careers for Numbers Crunchers
Careers for Sports Nuts
Careers for Travel Buffs
Guide to Basic Resume Writing
Handbook of Business and Management Careers
Handbook of Health Care Careers
Handbook of Scientific and Technical Careers
How to Change Your Career
How to Choose the Right Career
How to Get and Keep Your First Job
How to Get into the Right Law School
How to Get People to Do Things Your Way
How to Have a Winning Job Interview
How to Land a Better Job
How to Make the Right Career Moves
How to Market Your College Degree
How to Prepare a *Curriculum Vitae*
How to Prepare for College
How to Run Your Own Home Business
How to Succeed in Collge
How to Succeed in High School
How to Write a Winning Resume
Joyce Lain Kennedy's Career Book
Planning Your Career of Tomorrow
Planning Your College Education
Planning Your Military Career
Planning Your Young Child's Education
Resumes for Advertising Careers
Resumes for College Students & Recent Graduates
Resumes for Communications Careers
Resumes for Education Careers
Resumes for High School Graduates
Resumes for High Tech Careers
Resumes for Sales and Marketing Careers
Successful Interviewing for College Seniors

SURVIVAL GUIDES
Dropping Out or Hanging In
High School Survival Guide
College Survival Guide

VGM Career Horizons
a division of *NTC Publishing Group*
4255 West Touhy Avenue
Lincolnwood, Illinois 60646-1975